Bringing Home the Gold:
10 Keys to Winning
the Investment Decathlon

Bringing Home the Gold:
10 Keys to Winning the Investment Decathlon

Joseph L. Shaefer

Dow Jones-Irwin
Homewood, Illinois 60430

Project editor: Jean Roberts
Production manager: Stephen K. Emry
Jacket designer: Image House
Jacket photo: Comstock Inc./Tom Grill
Production services: Spectrum Publisher Services, Inc.
Typeface: 11/13 Century Schoolbook
Printer: Arcata Graphics/Kingsport

LIBRARY OF CONGRESS
Cataloging-in-Publication Data

Shaefer, Joseph L.
    Bringing home the gold: 10 keys to winning the investment
decathlon / Joseph L. Shaefer.
        p.   cm.
    Bibliography
    Includes index.
    ISBN 1-55623-161-X
    1. Stocks. 2. Speculation. 3. Investments. 4. Finance,
Personal.   I. Title.
HG6041.S44 1989
332.6'78—dc19   88–27473
                                                              CIP

Printed in the United States of America
1 2 3 4 5 6 7 8 9 0 K 6 5 4 3 2 1 0 9

To Jay N. Jay,
who done it

CONTENTS

The Advantages and Disadvantages of Mutual
Funds. Types of Mutual Funds. "Loads" (Sales
Charges). Investment Goals of Mutual Funds.
Schwab's Mutual Fund Marketplace.

Daily Sources of Information. Weekly Sources of
Information. Magazines and Newsletters. Books
on Investment. Other Sources of Information.

Stockbrokerage Firms. Financial Planners.
Investment Counselors.

The Securities and Exchange Commission. The
Self-Regulatory Organizations (SROs). The
Federal Reserve Board.

**CHAPTER 12 Winning: Five Events We Must
Master**   **173**

Buying and Selling Unpopular Common Stocks.
Buying and Selling Convertible Securities.
Selling Short. Buying and Selling Warrants,
SCOREs, "Long-Term" Options, and IPs.
Buying, Selling, and Switching Growth and
Total-Return Mutual Funds.

**CHAPTER 13 Knowing When to Make Your Move:
Timing Is Everything**   **201**

The Five Primary Market-Timing Tools. 10
Additional Market-Timing Tools. Stalking the
Wily Indicators.

**CHAPTER 14 Bringing Home the Gold—
Starting Today**   **212**

INTRODUCTION

BRINGING HOME THE GOLD

This is a book about investing intelligently in the stock market.

It's about making money and, once you've made it, keeping it.

It's written for you, the independent investor, who realizes that it's your money and it's your life, so you're the one who must take responsibility for your own investment success.

Our premise throughout the book is that there is nothing particularly complicated about success in investing—that, in fact, too many self-appointed "experts" complicate it unduly in order to convince you that you are incapable of directing your own investment destiny. The result is that there are a lot of spectators out there who take out of their investing exactly what they put in: nothing. If you've ever been one of those meek and trusting spectators who went to an "expert," hat in hand, and held out your wallet with a "please don't hurt me" look on your face, get ready to have some fun. This isn't a spectator sport—it's a participant sport. And you're about to learn the rules.

By the time you finish this book, you'll know how to distance yourself from the pack of also-rans that comprises most investors. The result will be exceptional reward and less risk than you're probably taking in your current investing. If you apply yourself diligently to understanding the rules of the game and then hone your strategy for playing it, the stock market is one game that rewards you with real gold.

I believe I can help you bring home that gold. I've been investing for more than 20 years, most of that time as an investment-industry insider. I began my career as a stockbroker with one of the oldest and biggest firms on Wall Street. After a number of years, I joined a discount brokerage firm in which I became the managing partner. I later sold that firm to Charles Schwab and, in the process, opened the first Charles

Schwab and Co. branch office in the eastern United States. I've been a branch manager and a regional manager, and I'm now a senior vice president with Schwab. I'm a Registered Principal, a Registered Options Principal, and a Financial and Operations Principal registered with the New York Stock Exchange.

Why is all this important to you? After all, you set out to read about successful investing, not to review my résumé. My background is important for one reason only: so that you know that I am an insider in the ways of Wall Street and when I tell you how it really works, I speak from long, sometimes arduous, but always fun and challenging personal experience.

If you're going to hire me—for the price of this book—to be one of your coaches, you need to know that I know the business from the inside out, that I know the competitors you'll be up against, and that I know the investing tricks of the trade that will allow you to distance yourself from those other competitors.

The strategies we'll discuss to make you a winning competitor have worked for me and for numerous other successful investors. Whenever I've stuck to my game plan, I've made money in the stock market. When I've strayed from these basic rules, I've lost money. My proposition to you is a simple one: when I've lost money, I've already lost it, so why don't I lose it for both of us? That is to say, since I've already made the mistakes, you don't have to. Isn't that what all player-coaches are supposed to do—pass on what worked in their playing career and advise you to avoid what didn't work?

We say the stock market is a game that rewards you with real gold, yet the stock market "game" itself is composed of a number of distinct competitive endeavors. Investing in the stock market is like an athletic competition in that both are organized games that pit individuals against other individuals. As in all such organized games, there are winners and there are losers. The winners will always be those who best understand the rules, the winning strategies, the way the games are scored, and the nature of the competition. Success in investing, as in any sport in which individuals compete against one another, consists of mastering the basics, matching skill and event, and knowing when to make the winning move. There is one sport that best typifies the myriad skills needed to succeed in the investment arena: the modern 10-event decathlon, which most of us have seen during the summer Olympics or at track-and-field competitions. Because there are 10 separate events, each requiring a very different set of skills to succeed, those who excel in the decathlon are those who have trained diligently and are adept in a number of key disciplines.

Just as in the decathlon, the stock market is first and foremost an *individual* effort. "Playing the market" is not a team sport. Make no mistake about it: no one else is on your side. The other players may not necessarily be against you, but they certainly are not *for* you. If you drop the ball, no teammate will be there to scoop it up for you. If you get lazy near the finish line, you can't rely on someone else to whisk the baton away from you and save the day. *You are on your own.* It is, therefore, in your best interest to prepare for the game completely and give it 100 percent.

The decathlon is also the ultimate test of the fittest and the fastest. Only the most competitive and best-qualified athletes—the best of the best—take on this rigorous event. The decathlon challenges us in 10 *different* skills: short runs such as the 100- and 400-meter events, longer runs like the 1,500-meter events, throwing weights (shot-put, discus, and javelin) or ourselves (high jumping, long jumping, and pole vaulting) the maximum distance we can, and a test of our skill in hurdling obstacles. *Many* different skills are needed to succeed at the decathlon, just as in investing. Anybody can play the market, but, just as in the decathlon, true success in the stock market requires that we excel in a number of different skills and bring them all together to achieve our own moments of glory.

Those who are Johnny One-Notes, good in only one event, seldom succeed. While you can invest for the sprint, the medium distance, or the long distance, you'd better be able to discern when to do which. Staying too long in a sour investment has turned many a quick profit into a serious long-term money-loser. While it's true that you're usually better off investing for the long run, in some cases it merely proves the validity of John Maynard Keynes's classic remark, "In the long run, we are all dead." Yet sprinting for a number of quick but small profits is almost never profitable. One big loser, and all those small profits are gone.

Being able to do different things at different times—in different markets—is the skill to develop. Make no mistake: there are just as many opportunities in bear markets as there are in bull markets—and with fewer competitors looking for those opportunities! Selling short, finding special situations and con-tracyclical stocks, and playing the convertible-securities or pre-cious-metals market can keep you a winner when others have thrown in the towel. It's consistency across a broad spectrum of events that equals success. Those who buy at the top, when all the news is good, or sell at the bottom, when the media panics them out, won't be competitors for long—which is why those who remain are very good indeed. The decathlon tests our ability to do a number of things well—not just one or two. Different kinds of investments work well at different times. We have to be good at *all* of them in order to succeed.

There's one other consideration that makes the decathlon an apt analogy. The decathlon stresses the basics. Remember, the skills it celebrates are skills human beings have needed to ensure their survival for untold centuries: *running,* either from something that wanted to eat them or after something that looked edible; *jumping,* either away from something that wanted to eat them or on top of something that looked edible and, once they got smarter, *throwing* something (from a safe distance) at anything trying to eat them or at something edible-looking trying to evade them.

Today it takes something different to survive: roughly the same instincts, but a weapon other than spears (or javelins), stones (or shot-puts), and fast feet (or fast feet). It takes gold. Whether dollars or marks or yen or kroner or cold hard cash, today survival means having money. And unless you're a rock star, oil-state sultan, or government contractor, you're not going to make it on your salary. You've got to get down on the field and make it in the competition.

Of course, there are some important differences between participating in the Olympic decathlon and investing in the stock market. In most decathlons, in theory anyway, only. amateurs may compete. In the stock market, amateurs are eaten for breakfast. Don't believe you are going to be the only one lucky enough to succeed on your good looks. No one, through pure luck, consistently succeeds in beating the pros. The pros became professionals because they knew they could be successful. You, too, must choose your coaches wisely, learn all you can, train diligently, and excel in the actual competition. In this game, amateurs need not apply.

Next, while the analogy of preparing for and winning our investing decathlon is a helpful one, remember that, unlike athletes, we are allowed to profit immediately from our success—we don't even have to wait for the product endorsements to roll in. Remember, too, that we are not merely running a race here, nor just competing in a decathlon. We are competing in a major life event—our future. We had better be ready to give it our best.

With this in mind, let's take a detailed look at this great game. In Part 1 we'll discuss the "precompetition training" needed to succeed: how we get in shape, the equipment we learn to use, the training that guides us along our way, the coaches and kibitzers, the referees, and the rule-setting organizations. Chapters 1–3 constitute an overview of basic investment alternatives and rationale. If you're an infrequent investor, read them carefully to get a strong grounding in the basics. If you're already comfortable with convertible preferreds, zero coupon bonds, 12b-1 fees on mutual funds, and all the other arcana of the game of investing, you might skim quickly through these first three chapters on your way to Part II, "Into the Blocks." (It's inevitable that, in discussing these key strategies, we may use terms that some readers aren't completely familiar with. In those cases, I've tried to recommend other readings that may be helpful. Conversely, some of the more basic information may be too basic for other investors. In either case, be persevering. The skills and strategies we will hone will benefit all investors— those who are new to the game as well as those who are much more experienced, those just starting out and those with large portfolios, individuals as well as professionals.)

In Part 2 we'll discuss the other players, peak performance, the 10 key events in which we will participate, the five primary timing indicators, and those strategies which result in failure, those which result in merely holding our own, and, most important, the winning strategies: those which bring home the gold.

PART 1

PRECOMPETITION TRAINING: TO PLAY THE GAME, KNOW THE EVENTS, KNOW THE RULES, KNOW THE SCORE

CHAPTER 1

WHO MADE THIS GAME UP?

Why There Are Stocks, Bonds, and All That Jazz

WHY THE GAME EXISTS

It's important that we remember *why* the game exists. In the decathlon, certain basic hunter/athlete skills are celebrated. In investing, we must be aware that stocks and bonds exist because there is a very real and pressing *need* for them. You get the opportunity to buy a stock because some person or persons, in the course of running their business, need more money than they can raise among themselves or from their friends or from their banker. They give up a small or big piece of ownership of their company in exchange for a small or big piece of your money. (*Note:* There is not always a direct correlation between how big a piece of ownership they give up and how big a piece of your assets they exchange it for!) Every stock traded today started in this manner. The United States wasn't the first nation with a stock exchange, but in the 1790s a few people got together and started trading new stocks under a buttonwood tree in what is now downtown Manhattan; in the 1890s American Telephone offered shares to the public; in the 1990s Hi-Tech Defense Electronics and Biotech Wonder Toys, Inc., may do so. In any case, the idea is the same: the company has grown about as much as it can on the capital it has. To get more, it offers shares to the investing public. By buying some of these shares on the "initial offering," you become a part owner of the company. Before you start feeling like a big-time corporate tycoon, however, remember that the company gives up only a *piece* of ownership in exchange for some of your money.

WHAT'S THE FIRST MOVE?

A public offering usually works something like this: three or four hotshot design engineers and maybe a marketing rep or two have been working for, say, IBM and one or two of its competitors for a few years. For whatever personal reasons, they become disaffected with the companies for which they work or think they can build a better mousetrap, or both. Heeding the call of the entrepreneurial siren, they, over a bottle of not-yet-expensive wine, talk one another into leaving their companies and setting up shop for themselves. Things go tougher for them than they expected, however, and they stumble along for a year or two with various "me-too" peripheral products, barely keeping their heads above water.

They still believe in their ability and their product or products though, and finally they come up with a real winner. Let's say this product is a 20-megabyte pocket-size personal computer. They know it will be a major breakthrough if only they can bring it into full-scale production, but they just don't have the capital to do so. They get together and decide to take out second mortgages on their homes and to tap all their friends and relatives. After doing so, they're able to come up with a prototype. By now, it's been two or three years since they left the occasional warmth and relative safety of their corporate womb, and Corporate Mom is beckoning more than a few of them to come home. In a last-ditch effort to stave off bankruptcy, they succeed in borrowing funds from a major bank. The bank makes the loan on the strength of the prototype but attaches all kinds of strings. Basically, all strings pull in the same direction: the engineers had better come up with a very marketable product very fast or see their family and friends become wards of the bank.

In a variation on this theme, a number of struggling entrepreneurial companies are not borrowing from banks but are seeking risk capital from *venture-capital firms*. This is a firm (or, occasionally, an individual) that takes the very large risk of providing funds to less-than-established companies in exchange for what it perceives to be *substantial* rewards somewhere down the road. Here, too, the venture capitalists are going to attach a number of strings to the deal. They may want to bring in professional outside management, have significant representation on the board of directors, determine salaries, or be given the right to hire and fire. Is this meddling? Is it meddling when the bank does it? It is and it isn't. Usually the venture-capital folks and the bankers have seen it all before and recognize the problems that face budding young companies long before the principals of the company are even aware that there *are* problems. Is it, however, *perceived* as meddling? Always. Often the principals, used to their freewheeling ways of doing things, will redouble their efforts just so they can get free of the venture capitalists and bankers. Whatever works.

In either case, whether they are indebted to the bank or bound by their agreement with the venture-capital firm, our engineer-entrepreneurs are mighty anxious to get out from under the debt. They do redouble their efforts and, lo and behold, they are successful. A finished pocket PC begins rolling off their production line, it's a hit at the trade shows, and orders start coming in. Are they out of the woods? Not by a long shot. Yes, they're making a profit on each computer they sell, but they can only make so many. After all, the pockets of the banks or venture capital firm were deep, but they weren't bottomless. Even with that much money, they had only enough funds to hire a half-dozen or so assembly technicians. They need five or ten times that many just to keep up with the current order flow. And they know that if they could hire more marketing people, they could sell even more product. And if they sell more, they know they'll need to hire more service technicians. And if their product can be copied by someone else, it shortly will be, so the time to strike is *now*. And if . . . And if . . .

About this same time, they face another dilemma. Either their banker is demanding something more than interest payments or their venture-capital firm is getting anxious to see some of that reward it anticipated when it took the risk of backing these untried computer wizards. Venture capitalists are not in business to marry one company for life; they are more interested in short-term meaningful relationships. Once they have seen what they feel is close to their maximum return, they don't want to stick around; after all, there are dozens of other young companies starting every day. Who knows? Maybe even some of the principals of *this* firm are already anxious to strike out on their own. Perhaps they didn't receive as high a management position as they felt they deserved, or maybe they just didn't get along with their peers, or maybe they wanted all the glory for themselves.

So our beleaguered engineers and sales people and technicians sit down with their banker or venture capitalist and start to thrash it out. Perhaps there is a lean and hungry *investment banking firm* involved with the company already. Even if not, after this meeting the company may begin contacting the various investment banking firms. The role of investment bankers is to advise the company on the best ways to raise additional money. They may recommend doing so through a *private placement* or a *bond offering* or any of a number of other avenues. Let's assume for now that they've recommended an initial public offering. Certain of their fees may be charged directly to the company, but, regardless, the investment bankers also charge the public, if indirectly, by buying the shares of this young company from the principals at one price, X, and selling the shares to the investing public at another price, X plus Y.

Is it fair that the investment bankers should "fix" the price like this? Sure. Why not? The investment banking firm, after all, does take 100 percent of the risk in introducing this untested company's shares to the public. The investment bankers should be, and are, allowed a reasonable reward. Plus, nobody's holding a gun to your head to buy the stock. (Well, except at *some* brokerage firms; we'll talk about *them* later.) The investment bankers consult with management, survey the prices and price-earnings ratios at which competing companies in the same industries went public and are currently trading, and try to come up with an *initial offering price* that will be so attractive that it will be an immediate sellout. The investment bankers effectively buy *all* of the stock that is to be offered to the public. The management of the company, who usually retain a significant share of ownership, have no further interest in those shares that have been purchased from the company by the investment bankers, but, since they still own many shares of stock, you'd better believe that they want the stock to rise. Since they probably kept a much bigger chunk than they sold, they, too, have a very real interest in the performance of the stock once it is publicly traded. It is incumbent upon the investment bankers to take all risks from this point on. They must resell to the public the shares that they purchased from the company. Remember, the investment banking firm is not in the business of holding large positions of diverse issues—that's what a *mutual fund* does. The investment bankers are in business to take what they hope is a well-defined risk, to hold the issue for the shortest possible time, to sell all shares to the investing public, and to move on to the next company ready to offer its shares to the public. This usually works in favor of the individual investor. Why? Because it is in the investment bankers' best interest to price the issue fairly in order to ensure that they themselves do not end up holding any of the shares. They are looking for an immediate sellout.

Does this mean that all new issues are good deals or are fairly priced? In a word, no. Often, entire industries are priced to sell at hope plus greed times infinity. In the post-Sputnik era, any issue with "science," "defense," or "electronics" in its name was priced in this manner. The great majority of these companies are no longer even in existence. It also happens that the investment bankers sometimes guess wrong on the demand for the issue and thus overprice it or that the company's management insists on a price higher than their investment banker recommended. Many new companies go belly-up within the same decade (occasionally within the same year) they are brought public, and most, at some point in their corporate existence, sell below their offering price—sometimes well below it. Despite this sad fact, many of them are offered initially at a price that is low enough, relative to others within the same industry, to go to a *premium* (a higher market price than the initial offering price) in at least the short term. Again, the investment banking firm *underwrites* (takes the risk in offering) the issue at a price that will guarantee that it sells. It doesn't want to be stuck with unsold shares of the company. It wants to buy these shares and quickly resell them to the public.

Unless the size of the potential *offering* is very small, no one investment banking firm actually shoulders the entire risk. Most often, the *lead underwriter* invites other investment banking firms to share the risk—and the potential rewards. They

jointly form an *underwriting group,* with the original investment banking firm—or another firm of their choosing—as the
managing underwriter. All these firms band together to put up
the money to buy the shares from the company. Thus, all of them
have the same interest in seeing these shares immediately re-
sold to the public at a tidy profit.

In order to ensure that all the shares are sold, the investment bankers want to get the word out to as many potential
buyers as possible. No matter how big these investment banking
firms are, they can't possibly reach all potential buyers themselves. As a result, the underwriters usually invite a number of
other brokerage firms to join them in selling the issue. These
other firms don't share in the risk of underwriting, so they do
not share in the underwriting profits. They do, however, become
a part of the *selling group* and are paid a predetermined commission for selling shares to the public. This commission comes out
of the underwriting group's total profits. On a large issue, as
many as 20 to 50 investment banking firms may be involved as
members of the underwriting group. Very often, these investment banking firms include the large retail brokerage firms
well known to most investors. These firms seek out investment
banking opportunities and sell the acquired shares to the investing public through their massive networks of retail stockbrokers. In addition, in a large public offering, there may be an
additional 30, 50, or 100 brokerage firms that do not have the
resources or the desire to be members of the underwriting group
but that are, nonetheless, members of the selling group.

When these shares are offered to you, the buyer, they are
offered at one fixed price. No additional commission charges are
tacked on. Before you interpret this as some type of windfall
from Wall Street, however, remember that you *are* paying a
commission. You are simply paying it in a different way—by
paying the markup between the price at which the underwriter
bought the shares and the price that you are paying to buy the
shares from the underwriter. Individual stockbrokers often try
to sell new issues by saying that there is "no commission" for
buying the security. Always remember that, while this may be
technically true, there's no such thing as a free lunch.

WHAT ABOUT BONDS?

The same thing occurs, by the way, when a company issues bonds and they are sold to you, the investor. They are offered at a *net price*—that is, with no extra commission charge—but don't believe the underwriter is doing you a favor. The underwriter's cut is reflected in the total price of the bond.

That said, what makes bonds different from stocks, and why would a company issue bonds rather than stocks? *Stocks* represent a piece of *ownership* of a company. If that company succeeds and grows and becomes the next IBM, you, as an owner, profit tremendously. But if they go bankrupt, you lose everything. You took on this risk when you decided to become a partial owner, which is just another way of saying you bought shares in the company.

When you buy a *bond,* however, you become, not an owner, but a creditor. There's a big difference in the type of investment you make, what your expectations are, and what the company owes you as a result. By analogy, if you were to give two friends $10,000 to start a retail store and they say that since you put up the money and they put up the work, then they will give you half the profits, that would be the equivalent, on a smaller scale, of buying stocks. In contrast, if you lend your friends $10,000 with the proviso that they pay you back the $10,000 with interest, that's the equivalent of buying a bond.

When you buy a bond, no matter how successful the company is, you do not share in their newfound prosperity (unless your bond is "convertible" into common stock, which we'll discuss in the next chapter). By the same token, no matter how poorly the company does (as long as they don't go bankrupt), the company still owes you the amount of money you effectively lent them by buying their bonds as well as the rate of interest they promised you when you bought them. (They actually still owe it to you even in bankruptcy. Being owed is not the same as getting, however.) If the company does go bankrupt, the bondholder has a claim against any assets the company may liquidate in bankruptcy. The holder of common stock does not. In addition to agreeing to pay you interest, usually semiannually, a company issuing bonds is promising—via their "bond" (or promissory note, if you will)—to repay all the money you initially invested at the original offering price. Since each bond usually has a *face value* of $1,000, the company is saying they will pay you, say, 20 years hence, your original $1,000 plus interest every year for the next 20 years. If they pay 10 percent per year, that would be $100 per year. Over 20 years, that would equal $2,000 in interest payments. That means you'd get interest of $2,000 and you'd get the $1,000 you originally "loaned" the company returned to you. Not bad, you say? Read on.

Remember, 20 years from now, $1,000 in *stock* in the same company could be worth zero dollars or $1,000 or $10,000 or, in unusual circumstances, even $100,000. If you are inclined to take the bird in hand—a $2,000 return on $1,000 invested in the bond—with the notion that while it isn't much, it's much safer than common stocks—remember to factor in inflation. Also remember that the bonds will go up and down in value relative to the interest rates prevalent at any given time. Don't forget the story about the man who falls asleep Rip Van Winkle–style and awakes in 20 years. He rushes to the telephone to call his stockbroker, who says, "Great news! While you were sleeping, your 1,000 AT&C went from $20 per share to $2,000 per share, your 500 Excor went from $38 per share to $4,000 per share, and your 600 Halox from $42 per share to $6,000 per share." Mr. Van Winkle has just time enough to say "Great! I'm rich, I'm rich!" before the operator cuts in and says, "Please deposit $100,000 for the next three minutes." At least stocks give you the chance to keep up with inflation, while bonds may or may not.

So let's look anew at the question, "Why are there bonds?" Imagine, if you will, that our exciting young company was successful in bringing shares public at $20 per share but that, since then, the market has declined, the computer industry is in a major slump, and the company has expanded too fast. Despite management's mistakes, the company is still quite solvent and in no danger of bankruptcy; but, as always, the market overreacts to exciting new products, concepts, and companies on the upside and overreacts to any real or perceived difficulties on the downside. The company needs money, but the company's shares, which management feels are worth at least $10 to $12 each, are selling for $6. The executive committee meets and says it is not about to effectively give away shares at $6 each—so it decides to issue bonds instead. A new company in an unpopular or poorly understood industry may be able to sell only bonds and then only to sophisticated institutional investors rather than the public. Why, you may ask, would a company put itself in debt via a promissory note when it could talk people into becoming owners and carry no obligations to repay the monies they put up? As the above example illustrates, there are bonds because companies are not always able to attract enough investors willing to become owners, but they can always find creditors—those who are willing to lend to it.

In the final analysis, there are stocks and bonds because companies need capital in order to grow, and investors provide that capital. Stocks and bonds are the two basic and standardized forms of evidence that you, the investor, have provided this capital, showing either ownership of the company or indebtedness to you by the company. In the next chapter we'll briefly discuss the various types of stocks and bonds, as well as how and where they are traded. We'll also discuss the "side bet" investments that have sprung up to enrich investors or stockbrokers or marketmakers (depending on whom you listen to)—warrants, PRIMEs and SCOREs, and their usually short-term cousins, stock and index options.

CHAPTER 2

CHOOSING OUR EVENTS: NARROWING DOWN A VERY BIG FIELD

Like the decathlon, modern investing can be described as consisting of 10 primary events, which we'll discuss in Part 2 of this book when we discuss winning strategies. Coincidentally, there are also 10 or so broad categories of possible investments. We can identify many more, but most of them are variations on these 10 basic themes. Some would add other types of investments to the following list, such as "investing" in commodities, futures, or options on commodities. I don't include them— but, then, I believe the term "investing" implies that you might actually see some of your money back someday!

So let's divide the various available investment alternatives into 10 broad categories:

1. *Common stocks.*
2. *Preferred stocks.* (Within this group are both preferred stocks and convertible preferred stocks.)
3. *Bonds issued by corporations.* Whether they are traditional bonds, "junk" bonds, convertible bonds, or zero coupon bonds, they're still debt instruments issued by corporations.
4. U.S. Treasury debt obligations, also known as *government securities,* or "guvvies." This classification, too, covers a lot of ground. These are not tax-exempt issues, but taxable debt instruments issued by the U.S. government, and they carry with them the U.S. government's obligation to repay them in full. As the pushy bond seller who calls you at home after dinner usually assures you, these securities are backed by "the full faith and credit of the U.S. government."

5. Bonds issued by various states, cities, and other governing agencies (excluding the federal government). These
are called *municipal bonds*. Municipal bonds are also
called tax-exempt bonds, for reasons we'll soon see.
6. *Warrants* to purchase common stock. Warrants give you
the right to purchase a certain number of shares of the
common stock of a company for a fixed period of time.
That period of time, however, usually is measured in
years, unlike options, for which the period of issue is
measured in months and the period of time the option is
held might be measured in hours or days.
7. *Options:* Equity options, or *stock options,* give you the
right to purchase or sell (depending on whether it's a
"call" or a "put") the underlying shares of common stock
from someone else (in the event of a purchase) or to
someone else (in the event of a sale) for a fixed period of
time, usually measured in months. *Index options* do not
represent underlying common stock in any one company. Rather, they represent ownership in a number of
underlying stocks. For instance, the Standard & Poor's
100 index option traded on the Chicago Board Options
Exchange represents ownership in 100 actively traded
listed issues. There are also indexes for individual industries and for precious metals, as well as for other
market proxies besides the Standard & Poor's 100.
8. *Index Participation Contracts.* This is a new type of
investment that combines certain features of both common stocks and index options. Like stock, Index Partic-
ipations (IPs) pay dividends, are marginable, and have
no expiration date. Like index options, the IP
represents a portfolio consisting of a broad-based market index, such as the Standard & Poor's 500 index.
9. PRIMEs and SCOREs. A relatively new product,
PRIMEs (Prescribed Rights to Income and Maximum
Equity) and SCOREs (Special Claim on Residual Equity) are derivative of the same concept that creates common stocks, though they are "packaged" differently.
Developed by an innovative outfit called the Americus
Shareowner Service Corporation, these instruments, by

creating a "unit" that duplicates the underlying common stock, effectively split stocks into two parts. The buyer of the PRIME receives all the dividends and has a "call" on the price appreciation *up to a fixed point*. The SCORE holder receives no dividend income but gets all price appreciation beyond that fixed point (the "termination claim" price). These instruments are issued for a fixed life of five years and are available on many of the bluest of the blue-chip stocks, including companies like IBM, General Electric, Ford, Sears, and General Motors. Recent tax rulings may limit the future availability of PRIMEs and SCOREs. Rather than attempt to predict the future direction of tax laws, however, we include these investments as examples of creative derivative instruments, possibly the first of many.

10. Mutual funds, both open-end and closed-end. We'll discuss mutual funds separately in Chapter 3, but to summarize here, both types of mutual funds offer similar advantages: diversification, professional management (whether that's an advantage or a disadvantage depends on who's doing the managing), and lower execution costs (because the funds buy in institutional-size quantities from their stockbrokers.) The disadvantages include the high sales commissions (also known as "loads") that some funds charge, the high fees that some funds charge to manage the funds, and, sometimes, the fund's management.

There are numerous themes and variations on these 10 categories. The only one of these variations that has had a truly major impact but is not included in our list is money market funds. Technically, these are mutual funds. What sets them apart is that they achieve diversification and professional management but invest primarily in short-term corporate and government debt obligations. They are mostly used by investors as a place to park between-investment funds.

There may be those who think that all bonds should be listed together as one "event," rather than discussed separately. After all, aren't all bonds purchased by investors seeking safety of capital, liquidity, and a guaranteed rate of return? By and large, it is true that investors purchasing debt obligations, whether from corporations, municipalities, or the federal government, are seeking those qualities. But just as, within the decathlon, there are 100-meter, 400-meter, and 1,500-meter runs, and they *are* all runs, each is a separate event designed to test each competitor across the full range of his or her skills. The reason we have chosen to look at the various bond types separately is that, depending on the individual investor's needs, each of these three types of bonds would be worthwhile for one part of his or her portfolio or at one point in his or her life to fulfill different investing strategies.

Let's look at the 10 broad categories of investment instruments in more detail and review the basics of buying securities on margin and on short selling. If you find *any* of these concepts alien to you, pick up a copy of Louis Engels' *How to Buy Stocks* for a quick refresher.

COMMON STOCKS

When people talk about "the stock market," what they are referring to, most of the time, are common stocks. *Common stocks* represent ownership in publicly traded companies. What that should imply, but all too often doesn't, is that common shareholders should consider themselves owners of the company, with all the *rights* and *responsibilities* that such ownership entails. For instance, it is said that the stockholders elect a board of directors to look out for their interests and to oversee the way in which the corporate officers manage the company. In fact, however, most shareholders don't view themselves as owners of the company, but as mere speculators—as spectators rather than participants in the decathlon. In fact, when a company sends proxies to elect directors (proxies give existing officers or directors the right to act "by proxy"—that is, to act on behalf of the shareholder), most shareholders don't even bother to fill them out and return them. All proxies not returned are, by default, voted by existing management, which allows management to vote those shares as they see fit.

We should never invest in common stocks merely as a speculation but should always consider that we are owners of that company. We should ask ourselves, if we had the opportunity to buy the entire company, would we? If the answer is, "No way!" then why are we speculating in this issue at all?

PREFERRED AND CONVERTIBLE PREFERRED STOCK

When we talk about the *equity* we have in our home, we're talking about ownership. If the price of that home were suddenly to plummet, we understand that we would lose our equity and possibly take a significant financial loss. Always remember that it's the same thing with the types of "equity" known as common stock, preferred stock, and convertible preferred stock. While common stock is the most popular of the three, it's important to remember that preferred stock and convertible preferred stock also represent equity—that is, ownership—with many of the same risks attendant on common-stock ownership. The primary difference is that shareholders owning *preferred stock,* as the name implies, receive preferential treatment in the event of a liquidation of the company. After (and only after) all debts, including debts to bondholders, are settled, the preferred shareholders have a first claim on whatever assets remain. The common shareholders, as always, would have whatever slim pickings remain after all debtholders *and* all preferred shareholders are taken care of. Because of this feature, many preferreds are purchased more for their yield and relative safety than for any other reason. And, in fact, most preferred stocks do not benefit as a result of a rise in the underlying common stock.

The exception to this rule is the *convertible preferred stock.* Convertible preferreds, as the name implies, give shareholders the right to convert their shares into a certain number of shares of the underlying common stock. On the one hand, these securities carry the promise of a certain dividend income. On the other hand, they do participate, in varying degrees depending upon the terms of the issue, in the appreciation of the underlying stock. This is because they carry an equity "kicker" with them—

they are "convertible" into shares of the underlying common stock. As an example, if each convertible preferred share cost us $15, yielded 8 percent, and was convertible into one share of common stock, and if the common stock yielded 0 percent (paid no dividend) and sold for $12, we'd hardly be interested in "converting" our shares into common stock. We'd immediately lose $3 per share and the 8 percent dividend income. However, if the underlying common stock rises in value to $24, our convertible preferred has to be worth *at least* $24 (since we could convert, share for share, into common) and, given the extra yield on the convertible preferred (remember, the common pays no dividend at all), will most likely have risen to *more than* $24.

If the common stock declines, the convertible preferred seldom declines as much. This is because the convertible preferred almost always pays a dividend, and this dividend is almost always greater than the dividend the underlying common stock pays. To continue our example, if the common stock declines 50 percent from $12 to $6, the preferred stock will not fall as far, percentagewise, as the common stock. If the convertible preferred goes to $7.50 per share, it will then be yielding 16 percent. (To yield 8 percent at $15, the convertible preferred will be paying a $1.20 dividend. If it declines to $7.50 per share and is still paying this $1.20 dividend, it will then yield 16 percent.) Unless interest rates are so high that 16 percent is no longer an attractive rate of return, it is unlikely that the convertible preferred will sink this far.

If it sounds as if convertible preferred stocks give investors the best of both worlds, why don't more people invest in them? The fact is that convertible preferreds are poorly understood by most investors, and they do have certain features that in some instances make them less attractive. Most preferreds, whether convertible or not, carry a provision that allows the company to call in the preferred at a time and place of its choosing. Why would it do this? Because the interest rate environment or the price of the underlying common has changed to the point where the company believes it can replace that issue with something that will allow it to pay a lower rate of interest. The other primary problem with convertible preferred securities is that they usually trade at a premium over their conversion value.

Conversion value is the price at which the convertible preferred can be converted into common stock. In our example, in which each share of preferred stock gave the shareholder the right to buy one share of common stock, we said that if the common were at $12, it's likely that each preferred share would trade above $12—$15 per share, in the example. This extra cost is called the *conversion premium.* It represents the additional price investors are willing to pay in order to obtain (usually) higher income on the convertible preferred and (always) preferential treatment in the event of a liquidation.

Even with these two potential drawbacks, the astute investor, wishing to maximize his or her returns, is well advised to investigate whether the security he or she is considering investing in also has a convertible preferred outstanding.

BONDS

Moving on to the various types of bonds, we need to keep it simple and remember that a *bond* is nothing more than physical evidence that we have "loaned" a company a sum of money. By purchasing the company's bonds, we become its creditor. The company, in turn, agrees to repay that money and to pay us interest on it. The corporate bond market is a very large one. In this age of institutionally dominated investing, most of the capital required to run today's large businesses comes from the bond market. The total amount of funds invested in the bond market is many times larger than the total invested in the stock market. Sometimes, corporations issuing bonds are able to sell their entire bond issue to just one or two or three large institutions. These institutions consist of the large banks, pension funds, insurance companies, and other large organizations that pool the capital of hundreds or thousands of smaller investors under the aegis of one institution.

We have said that common stockholders look for an increase in the value of their ownership stake, whereas bondholders look primarily for the safety of their principal and a fixed return. This means that bonds usually fluctuate less than common stocks. In periods of rapidly rising or falling interest rates, however, bondholders have been known to take a wild and woolly ride as well. For instance, if in one year a company issues a bond paying 6 percent interest, and five years later that same company, in a different interest rate environment, needs funds, it may have to issue the bond to yield 12 percent rather than 6 percent. This would occur if interest rates were generally high and, in order to be competitive in placing its bond issues in the hands of institutional or individual investors, the company had to pay what everyone else was paying. If you were able to lend money and receive 12 percent interest somewhere else, you'd be unlikely to accept less than 12 percent from this company. Well, when that happens, what fate befalls the bonds issued five years earlier, at 6 percent? Before you'd invest $1,000 in that previously issued bond and get $60 a year in interest (6 percent), you'd buy the newer one for $1,000 in order to get $120 per year (12 percent). As a result, the older bond will decline in price to roughly half of the $1,000 it was issued at, or $500—at which price, since it still pays $60, it will also yield 12 percent. As long as the bond has a number of years remaining until maturity, this will be true. As it approaches maturity (the date the company repays the entire principal amount), it will, of course, come closer and closer in value to the $1,000 the company will pay to "redeem" it from you.

Since the company issuing bonds and common stock recognizes that bonds represent an obligation that *must* be repaid, whereas common stock represents a way of raising capital that does not incur any obligation other than the implied obligation to attempt to run the company successfully and at a profit for all owners, why would any company obligate itself to repay debt? Why not just issue common stock? The reasons are twofold. In the first place, as we mentioned earlier, unless the company is *exceedingly* well thought of, debt obligations may be the only kind of capital the company can raise. Most investors, and particularly the institutional investors who dominate the capital markets, are unwilling to take an ownership position of any size in any but the most solid of companies. The other reason a company might choose to issue a debt obligation is that, when a company makes interest payments on a bond issue, this is considered a cost of doing business on the company's books and is therefore deducted from the company's published earnings before the company figures its federal and state income taxes. Any dividend the company pays on its common stock, in contrast, comes out of the earnings the company declares after it has paid all its debt obligations and other costs of doing business as well as its federal and state income taxes.

CORPORATE BONDS

In the world of *corporate bonds,* there are three kinds of "straight" bonds (as opposed to convertible bonds) that you will encounter. The most common is called a *debenture.* A debenture is backed by the full faith and credit of the corporation but is not secured by any particular piece of property or other asset the corporation owns. A *first mortgage bond* is a bond secured by a mortgage on the company's various assets in the aggregate. *Equipment trust certificates* are obligations that are secured by specific pieces of equipment. Thus, an equipment trust certificate might be secured by an airline's fleet of six 747 jet aircraft. Since the aircraft are protected by insurance in the event of catastrophic loss, the only risk in this kind of bond is that the value of the equipment will fall below a level that will allow the company to repay each debtholder or bondholder his or her principal at maturity.

CONVERTIBLE BONDS

Companies and investment bankers realized many years ago that some investors wanted the security of a debt obligation but still wanted the fun of having an ownership kicker, so they began to issue convertible bonds as well as convertible preferred stocks. *Convertible bonds,* like convertible preferreds, give bondholders the right to exchange ("convert") their bonds for a certain number of shares of the underlying common stock. The convertible bondholder has the company's promise, in the form of the bond, that it will pay a fixed rate of return every year. Since most bonds are issued at $1,000, an 8 percent convertible bond will pay $80 per year, a 9 percent bond $90, and so on. While convertible bonds pay the debtholder a certain rate of interest, it is virtually always a lower rate than they would receive had they elected instead to take a straight (nonconvertible) bond. This is because the company has also provided that equity kicker we discussed in the section on convertible preferred stocks. Because we buyers of convertible bonds have the opportunity to participate in the price appreciation of the underlying common stock, we are willing to accept a slightly lower rate of return on our "loan" to the company than we otherwise might have. Should the value of the underlying common stock rise, we will often benefit to a great degree, since we may convert our bond into common stock. All the benefits, and the few disadvantages, of convertible preferred stocks apply to convertible bonds as well. While bonds are the more "senior" (more desirable in the event of a corporate bankruptcy), when we talk later about the benefits and uses of "convertibles," we will be referring to *both* convertible bonds and convertible preferred stocks.

GOVERNMENT BONDS

It's probably safe to say that virtually every investor in America has purchased a *government bond* at one time or another, whether he or she knew it or not. The Series E savings bond that many of us received at birth from doting relatives are true government bonds. We also indirectly own government bonds if we have a money market fund. While most money market funds try to maximize their return by purchasing corporate rather than government obligations, most of them at any given time have some short-term government obligations in their portfolios. A third way many of us own government bonds, if indirectly, is through our investment in stock or income mutual funds. When you read that a mutual fund has a cash position of 10 percent of its portfolio, that doesn't mean that they're 90 percent invested in stocks and have 10 percent sitting around in 10 and 20 dollar bills. That 10 percent is invested in what are known in the industry as *cash-equivalent securities*. Although these securities are referred to as "cash," they are, in fact, usually very short-term government or corporate obligations.

Finally, most of us who work for companies that have their own pension funds are indirect owners of government bonds. Pension-fund managers, with a charter to protect those funds so that they are available to us at retirement, seek the safest possible investment choices for a good portion of their funds. What this often means is at least some investment in government bonds. We use the term "bond" generically in this case—in fact, there are a number of different alternatives. Some individual investors and institutions purchase U.S. Treasury bills, some of which mature in as little as three months and a day. Others purchase U.S. Treasury notes, which have maturities of up to seven years. And still others purchase U.S. Treasury bonds, which have maturities ranging from five years on up to 30 years or so. In addition, included in the government securities marketplace are bonds issued by various government agencies, such as the Government National Mortgage Association (GNMA) and Federal Home Loan Banks. These issues are traded under such colorful names as Ginnie Maes, Sally Maes, Fannie Maes, and Freddie Macs. (You have to remember that government bond dealers don't always get a whole lot of excitement in dealing with something as staid and relatively secure as government bonds. To add some color to an occasionally drab marketplace, they *had* to do stuff like this.)

Even though these obligations have behind them the full faith and credit of the U.S. government, between the time they are issued and the time they mature, they, too, are subject to massive interest rate fluctuations. A great deal of money can now be made or lost in trading government securities. The only security here is that, if we hold on until maturity and if the U.S. government is still capable of paying its obligations, we will receive full principal value at maturity. (Of course, if the U.S. government is *not* capable of paying its bills, then probably all other securities in this country and every other country are worthless as well and this book won't be any help to you. While that thought may sell lots of gloom-and-doom books, the odds of it occurring are minuscule. For as long as there have been securities markets—indeed, as long as there have been gov-

ernments—people have been predicting the decline of civilization as we know it. Miraculously, we humans, being the remarkably adaptive creatures that we are, muddle through to even
greater successes. My assumption throughout this book is that
we will continue to do so—*and the times that most people are
convinced that we will not make it are the times of greatest
opportunity*.)

MUNICIPAL BONDS

The last type of bond we'll look at is the *municipal bond*. Interest
paid on municipal bonds is exempt from federal income taxes, so
these bonds are also called *tax-exempt bonds*. As a result, municipal bonds are best suited for those investors whose income
places them in the highest federal income tax brackets. Given
that there are close to 100,000 states, counties, cities, and sub-
units of local governments and that most of them have issued
bonds at one time or another, there are plenty of choices available. These governing bodies need money for hospitals, housing,
transportation networks, schools, and other components of the
infrastructure and services that all of us have come to expect
from various government entities. In addition to the federal tax
exemption, interest on the obligations of a number of states is
also exempt from taxation. That means that if an investor in
California purchases a State of California obligation, he or she
will have to pay no federal or state tax on the interest received
on that bond. Though there are a number of different names and
indeed a number of different types of municipal bonds, the two
most common are general-obligation bonds and revenue bonds.
General-obligation bonds, which constitute the great bulk of
municipal bonds, are backed by the full faith and credit of the
issuing entity. Remember, most of these entities also have tax-
ing power, which guarantees them a much better stream of
income than you or I are guaranteed and therefore usually
makes them a better investment risk. *Revenue bonds* are issued
to finance specific undertakings like the building of a new hos-
pital or a new toll road. The principal is secured by these specific
undertakings, and the interest is paid only from the revenues
collected by them. There are other types of municipal bonds,

such as housing authority bonds and industrial revenue bonds. These are also tax-free but are not nearly as popular as the other two types.

ZERO COUPON BONDS

In all these types of bonds—corporate, government, and municipal—there is an interesting subset called *zero coupon bonds*. (There's even a "zero" for convertible bonds, called a Liquid Yield Option Note, or a LYON). "Zeros" are bonds that are issued at a significant discount from face value and that do not pay regular interest but promise to pay their full $1,000 face value at maturity. They can be secured with a very small investment, usually 10 cents or 20 cents on the dollar for a 20-year or so obligation, and are particularly beneficial when we expect to need funds, say for a college education or retirement, X number of years down the road.

We now leave the better-known areas of stocks and bonds, with all their combinations and permutations, for a look at the various "side bets"—that is, those investment opportunities which were created by companies to add value to their stock and bond offerings, like "warrants," and those not issued by the companies themselves but rather created to take advantage of the marketplace that exists after those issues have been brought public. Examples of this latter group include stock options, index options, and open-end and closed-end mutual funds.

WARRANTS

Warrants to purchase shares of underlying common stock have been around for a long time. They have, however, recently been overshadowed by their newer upstart cousins, stock options and index options. Ever since stock and index options gained prominence in the 1970s, warrants have often been overlooked in favor of options. Yet, in many ways, warrants have all the benefits of options with few of the disadvantages.

Warrants offer the right to purchase shares of common

stock directly from the company itself. Warrants are often issued in conjunction with a bond offering or a private placement of bonds or, occasionally, with common stock as a "sweetener"—a way of making the purchase of those bonds or shares more attractive to the purchasers.

Don't confuse the issuance of warrants with the concept of a convertible bond or a convertible preferred stock. Warrants issued in all these circumstances trade completely separately from, for instance, the bond issue with which they were originally issued. They were most likely "thrown in" because, while the potential investors wanted the safety and senior debt status of a bond, they had a number of bond issues to choose from. In many cases, other issuers might have had the edge in safety or reputation. As a result, or perhaps because our company wanted to pay a guaranteed rate of interest slightly less than the existing market rate, the company issued warrants as well. These warrants then give the holder the opportunity to participate to some extent should the underlying common stock do well.

For instance, a company whose shares trade at $18 a share may issue a bond in an environment where other bonds from companies like itself are yielding 8 percent. Our company brings its issue to yield only 7.85 percent but also sells, with each bond, 100 warrants, or rights to purchase its common stock at a price of $28. What does this do for the company? It allows the company to issue debt obligations at a slightly better interest rate than it might have and it also, should the stock do well, allows the company to, in effect, sell shares of stock to the public at $28 without reregistering for a public offering. Remember, after a company's stock is already publicly traded, even if it goes from $18 to $28, the company normally does not benefit from this stock price increase. The *shareholders* benefit, which in turn makes them very happy with the company's management, which in turn may make them more agreeable when the company's management votes itself bonuses, stock options, company cars, and other worldly goods. In the case where the company has warrants outstanding, however, when the warrants increase in value and are exercised, the company actually has the opportunity to raise additional capital (as well as give great bonuses, company cars, and raises to its senior executives)!

Many warrants trade at no higher a premium (the difference between their exercise value and the price at which they are trading) than an option would. Yet options are only good for, at best, a few months, whereas some warrants are good for many years and a few are granted in perpetuity. Should you find a company in whose prospects you believe strongly, we've already suggested that you consider purchasing its convertible preferred stock or convertible bonds. To that we now add that you should also consider purchasing warrants on that company. If the company were trading, as in our earlier example, at $18 per share and a six-month option to purchase it at $25 was selling for $1 and a nine-month option to purchase it at $25 were selling at $2, the warrant to purchase it at $28, good for another 10 *years,* might be selling for only $4. If you believed strongly in the prospects of this company, but weren't convinced that it would realize its full potential in the next six or nine months, it would be smarter to buy the warrant.

If, at the time the warrant to buy at $28 expired, the underlying common stock was selling at $28 or less, your warrant would expire worthless—that is, you'd have a 100 percent loss of your invested capital. If, however, the warrant were trading at any point above $28 at expiration, you would have some of your capital returned or have a profit. If, for example, it were selling at $30 at expiration, your warrant would be worth $2, since you could buy a $30 stock for $28 plus one warrant. If it were selling at $32, your investment would be worth $4—exactly what you paid for it. If you had been correct in assessing this company and its common stock had gone from $18 up to $28 up to $38, your warrant would be worth $10, for a 250 percent return. At any time prior to expiration of the warrant, even though it has no "intrinsic value" (the "real" value of the warrant, reflecting the difference between the price at which the warrant may be exchanged for common stock and the current market price of that stock), it will still have a "time value" based on other investors' and speculators' belief that the stock has further appreciation potential.

There are warrants on companies in virtually every industry as well as on precious-metal stocks and different currencies. (By buying or selling "currency exchange warrants," you can speculate on the future direction of various countries' currencies—more on this in Chapter 12.)

Warrants, just like stocks and bonds, trade in the secondary market. As a result, you don't have to purchase the bond they were originally issued along with in order to buy and sell the warrants. The bonds trade in one market, and the warrants trade in another. Many of the persons or institutions who receive the warrants along with the bonds choose to sell their warrants in order to effectively increase the yield on their investment.

OPTIONS

Options are such a potentially complicated tool that they deserve a book of their own—and there have been dozens of books written on understanding the options market and, theoretically at least, profiting from it. More information and misinformation (mostly the latter) has probably been written about listed options than any other single investment alternative ever enjoyed in *its* first 15 years of existence. Probably the best basic piece on the subject is published by the Options Clearing Corporation and is titled *Risks and Characteristics of Listed Options*. If you haven't read this pamphlet (available from any broker or any exchange that trades listed options), do so. Until you understand the contents of this pamphlet, *especially the sections on risk,* you should stay away from the options market.

The best way to think of how options work is by using a real-estate analogy. Let's say that you own a farm 20 miles outside of a major metropolitan area. You read in the papers that the state is considering a new freeway that will connect your metropolitan center with another 40 miles away. Your land and that of your neighbor are directly in the path of the proposed freeway. Should the freeway be built, you and your neighbor both stand to gain from all those oil companies and fast-food chains that will want to snap up your land at double its current value. Let's say that you believe that this freeway will be built but that your neighbor doesn't agree. If you go to your neighbor, knowing that his land, pre-freeway, is worth $100,000 and you offer him $5,000 for the right to purchase his property for $100,000 at any time in the next six months, you've just bought yourself an option. Since the decision is expected on the freeway within the next three months, you figure you're pretty smart. If the freeway doesn't get built, you've lost $5,000. But if the freeway does get built, you may have made the difference between the $5,000 you paid and the upwards of $200,000 the property is now worth. Not a bad risk–reward relationship: $5,000 risked for a potential $100,000 reward.

If you *don't* believe the freeway will be built, you might, like your neighbor, sell the option on your property to someone else. Again, since you don't think the freeway will ever be built, you look at the $5,000 as found money. In the unlikely event that the freeway is built, well, you figured $100,000 was a fair price for your land anyway.

The first example, in which you paid your neighbor $5,000 for the right to purchase his property, is the equivalent of buying an option in the stock market. The second example, in which you sold someone else the right to purchase your property, is the equivalent of selling, or "writing" an option in the stock market. In both cases, the dollar amount, $5,000, is considered the *premium*. If you are the buyer, we say that you have paid a $5,000 premium for the right to purchase that property within the next six months. If you are the seller, you have received $5,000 in premium income for giving up the *potential* future use of your property. The $100,000 is the *exercise price,* or the *strike price*— the price at which you would strike a deal and exercise your option. In the stock options market and index options market, just as with our real-estate example, you need not, of course, wait until the six months (or three months, or nine months, or whatever the term of your option is) to sell it. You may purchase and sell options at any time during their life. Stock options are written to expire in three, six, or nine months, while index options expire more frequently.

Thus far we have talked about buying "*call*" options. That is to say, we buy an option which allows us to profit if the underlying security rises in value. We can also play the other side of the market by purchasing "*put*" options, which are simply options that you purchase in the belief that the price of the stock represented by those options will decline, rather than increase, in value. Put options trade the same way as call options, and with virtually the same liquidity. The amount of premiums charged to purchasers and received by sellers is based purely on supply and demand. If many more persons wish to purchase call options than there are at that moment sellers wishing to sell those options, the premiums will grow larger, or "widen." The same is true with puts, of course. Remember, when we talk about selling puts or calls, just as in the example we used with our two landowners, we are talking about writing those options for the first time. In the options market, this is called "selling to open" a position. The purchaser is "buying to open" a position. When the seller of those options chooses, before expiration, to close out his or her position, he or she is said to "buy to close." Conversely, when the purchaser of an option buys to open and then chooses to sell his or her position, he or she is said to "sell to close." In short, the purchaser "buys to open" and "sells to close," while the seller "sells to open" and "buys to close."

Straddles

A *straddle* is nothing more than the purchase *or* sale of a put and a call at the same time on the same stock. So, for example, if we believe that a certain volatile stock will jump one way or the other by a great deal, we might buy a put on the stock at, say, $20 per share and a call on the stock, also at $20 per share. If the stock happened to be right at $20, it might cost us, let's say, $200 as a *premium* for the put and a $200 premium for the call. Our total investment is thus $400 (plus commissions). If the stock moves below $16 *or* above $24, we will begin to have a profit. Our bet when we straddle a stock is that the stock will move significantly. We don't really care in which direction it moves. We do care, however, that it makes this move before a certain date—the dates at which our options expire.

Of course, those who write options instead of purchasing them can also write a straddle. In this case, the same dynamics apply. The stock must move beyond $16 or $24 before they have, effectively, a loss. The seller is betting that the stock will trade in a broad range of between $16 and $24. The buyer is betting that the stock will trade well beyond the range of $16 to $24.

Spreads

Just as a straddle is the simultaneous *purchase* of *both* calls and puts or the simultaneous *sale* of *both* calls and puts, a *spread* is the simultaneous *purchase and sale* of *calls* or the simultaneous *purchase and sale* of *puts,* always of the same underlying security. Now, we could get carried away discussing the various types of spreads: people talk about their butterfly spreads and their sandwich spreads and all other manner of flora and fauna, but, in fact, they are all variations on three basic types. The first of these is a *calendar spread.* A calendar spread is nothing more than two options that have identical strike prices and different expiration dates. For example, a calendar spread might be established on the March calls or puts with a strike price of 60 that gives us the right to buy the underlying shares of XYZ Corp. (the March 60 XYZs) and the June calls or puts with a strike price of 60 (the June 60 XYZs). Usually you write the option with the closer expiration date and purchase the one that is further away.

The second type of spread, an *exercise price spread,* consists of a long option at one strike price and a short option at another, usually expiring the same month. The exercise price spread is considered a *bull spread* when you have purchased the lower of the exercise prices and written the higher one. For instance, a bull spread might be a purchase of the aforementioned March 60 XYZ call and the sale at the same time of a March 65 XYZ call. A *bear spread* is established when you do just the opposite: sell the March 60 XYZ call and buy the March 65 XYZ call.

Finally, a *combination spread* is any spread that consists of buying options at one exercise price and expiration date and selling options with a different exercise price and expiration date. Thus, a combination spread might be the purchase of the March 60 XYZ calls and the sale of the June 65 XYZ calls.

Since I refuse to make this subject any more complicated than it already is, I've chosen not to discuss butterfly or sandwich spreads, call ratio backspreads, strangles, and all the other arcane paraphernalia that certain investment professionals have established to increase their income by separating you from some of yours. If you are genuinely interested in these strategies, I suggest you purchase a seat on one of the options or futures exchanges. That's because these strategies were designed for those who can devote virtually all their time and attention to them. Anyone not heeding this advice and rushing headlong into these things, especially with the gleeful cooperation of a commission-hungry broker, deserves what he or she gets, which is to be butterflied, spread, stripped, strapped, boxed, straddled, and strangled.

INDEX OPTIONS

We've been talking about options that have underlying common stocks. There are also options that give us the right to purchase or sell (call or put) not an individual stock, but a whole basket of stocks. These are collectively called *index options*. There are as many combinations and permutations of index options as there are brokerage firms, specialists, and marketmakers eager to find new and exciting ways to keep you from getting bored or rich.

There are indexes on the Standard & Poor's 100, the Standard & Poor's 500, the Value Line Composite, the Major Market Index, the Institutional Index, the New York Stock Exchange Index, the Financial Composite Index, as well as numerous industry indexes such as those for gold and silver, computer technology, oil, and utilities. I am not suggesting that you avoid all of these, merely that you wait until you can demonstrate to yourself that you can make a reasonable rate of return for at least two years running in equity options before plunging head-first into the potential crevasses awaiting you in index options.

INDEX PARTICIPATION CONTRACTS

Index Participation Contracts (IPs) offer the independent investor a less risky way to play "the market." There is less risk in IPs than in index options, greater flexibility and the same degree of diversification. Unlike index options, IPs have no strike price and no expiration date. They are, effectively, a proxy for buying a broad-based portfolio of a number of stocks. As the underlying issues comprising this portfolio pay dividends, they will be passed through to the holders of the IP on a quarterly basis. Given all these characteristics, IPs make much more sense for almost all independent investors than the considerably more risky index options.

PRIMEs AND SCOREs

"Issued" by the Americus Shareowner Service Corporation and trading on the American Stock Exchange, *PRIMEs* and *SCOREs* have been an innovative investment alternative. The operant words here are "have been." Basically, what Americus has done is to create "trusts" for 27 blue-chip securities. They then invite shareholders in these 27 companies to exchange shares for units consisting of both PRIMEs and SCOREs, the theory being that the sum of the parts will be worth more than the whole. The problem is that the various tax "reforms" have effectively quashed these types of transactions by changing the tax status of the exchange and subsequent sale and by ruling that fixed investment trusts may no longer have multiple forms (like having both PRIMEs and SCOREs). Given that this now becomes a taxable event for shareholders, anyway, it's unlikely that additional trusts will be created in the future.

Nonetheless, there are two important reasons for discussing PRIMEs and SCOREs here. One is that they are truly innovative products that offer a unique investment opportunity for the sharp investor, at least until the last of them expire in 1992. And the other reason is that, as the president of Americus said recently, "The genie is out of the bottle." He couldn't be more right. Investors have shown that they're interested in products like this, and it's only a matter of time before Americus or someone else comes up with a variation on this theme that gets past the scrutiny of the IRS. With all this in mind, let's take a look at this type of investment.

Remember, PRIMEs and SCOREs appeal to two completely different types of investor. People who want the safety and security of their blue-chip stock will want to purchase the prime unit. The PRIME unit entitles them to receive all dividends paid by the company as well as a call on a small amount of appreciation in the underlying common stock. Thus, a retired person who wants income but also wants to participate to at least a small degree in the underlying appreciation of their blue chips might purchase a PRIME.

The purchaser of a SCORE is willing to give up any dividend income and is also willing to give up the first few dollars of appreciation in a stock. What the SCORE purchaser is buying is a warrant, or a call, or a long-term option, on the success of that underlying company beyond the fixed price up to which the PRIME holder benefits.

As an example, if Blue Chip, Inc., had units issued by Americus split into PRIMEs and SCOREs, and was paying a dividend yield of 8 percent at $50 per share, the PRIME holder might have the privilege of getting that 8 percent dividend for as long as the company paid it and until the expiration of the PRIME and might also receive the benefit of any appreciation in the stock up to, say, $55. The PRIME holder would also have the risk of the decline in the value of the PRIME, theoretically to zero, just as he or she would if they held the common stock. The purchaser of the SCORE might purchase the SCORE for around $10. That SCORE would expire worthless when the unit representing both the PRIME and the SCORE expired five years down the road unless the common stock were worth more than $55. At $54 the SCORE is worthless and the SCORE holder has received no income whatsoever during the time he or she has held it. At 55⅛, the SCORE holder has something worth one-eighth. If it sounds like most of the benefits accrue to the PRIME holders, hang on. Let's suppose that the underlying stock, Blue Chip, Inc., was in the business of making automobiles. Let's further suppose that the auto industry had been depressed for a period prior to the issuance of PRIMEs and SCOREs. Should that situation turn around and our underlying stock appreciate to $100 on the basis of earnings and future prospects, the holders of the PRIME may be kicking themselves for missing all that appreciation (although they did get their guaranteed participation up to $55 and their dividends). The SCORE holders, however, had an opportunity to play Blue Chip, Inc., for $10 instead of

$50 and saw that $10 go up in value to $45. Had they purchased the common stock, they would have had more dividend income, but only a 200 percent profit—and that 200 percent would have required a cash outlay of $5,000. By purchasing the SCORE, they had a cash outlay of only $1,000 and a rate of return of 450 percent over the same period of time. PRIMEs and SCOREs are another opportunity we'll talk more about when we discuss winning strategies.

MARGIN ACCOUNTS

Before we end this chapter, let's review two techniques often used in conjunction with the investment alternatives just mentioned: short selling and buying on margin.

Buying on margin is one way to leverage your investments so that, if they do well, you can increase your profits at a faster rate than you would have otherwise. Conversely, if the stocks you buy drop in value, your personal loss is far greater.

Brokerage firms are usually quite willing to extend credit so that you can buy on margin. That's because they get to act like a bank when you buy on margin, making a profit by acting as the middleman while lending you other people's money. When a bank "accepts" your checking deposit and pays you 0 percent on your credit balances (or takes in your savings account deposit and pays you 5½ percent), it then turns around and lends that money out to others at whatever rate the market will bear. Given a prime rate of, say, 8½ percent (the *prime rate* being the rate at which banks lend money to their lowest-risk corporate customers), the bank's average return on its portfolio, even after allowing for losses because of its own bad judgment in granting high-risk loans, is likely to be very substantial. Not a bad business, that. Pay one person 5½ percent or less and lend it to someone else at 9 or 10 percent. Do that, on a few hundred million dollars, always using other people's money, and you'll see why banks have all that plush carpeting and expensive art and furniture.

Like banks, brokerage firms also like the idea of lending out other people's money. The Glass-Steagall Act prevents brokerage firms from accepting checking deposits, so they've found another way to accept "deposits" and to lend money. They simply take all the "free credit" balances (monies left in customers' accounts, funds received by brokers for customer sales not yet paid to customers, and the like) on which they usually pay their customer 0 percent, and they also take all the in-house money market fund or asset-management account dollars (on which they pay a sliding scale which, for illustration purposes, we'll say this week is blended at 7 percent), and then they lend these funds out to margin-account buyers at 9 percent or so. A number of brokerage firms have in excess of $1 billion in outstanding margin loans. At even a 1 percent spread between cost of funds and funds lent, that's $10 million income with virtually no risk. Not a bad business to be in. . . .

For this reason, some brokers will suggest that you treat a margin account as a place to get a low-cost loan. After all, their logic goes, "You buy your house on credit, buy a car on credit, and use credit cards for many other purchases. Why pay 15 percent or 18 percent on a credit card when we'll lend you the money at only 9 percent?" The answer is that, while houses and cars and VCRs go down in value, they seldom lose 50 percent of their value in a single day. Individual stocks conceivably could, and sometimes do. It's no fun when your brokerage firm issues a margin "maintenance call," telling you that if you don't deposit cash or other marketable securities immediately, any remaining stocks in your account will be sold down to the point where the broker has secured its loan to you. This often creates a "waterfall" effect and forces individuals to sell at exactly the time they would rather be buying.

Yet there is a time to buy on margin. Remember, the Federal Reserve Board determines the "initial margin requirements" but each brokerage firm determines its own "maintenance requirements" (though these requirements are always at least as high as the New York Stock Exchange's 25 percent minimum maintenance requirements). This means that I can buy 200 shares of a $30 stock for $3,000 on margin, only 100 shares if I pay cash. If the stock should fall below $22.50 per share and if my brokers have a 35 percent maintenance requirement, they'll want more money from me. That's because, of my $3,000 investment, my portion of the account (remember, my brokers effectively own the rest of the account until I repay my loan to them) is now worth only $1,500, and that's less than 35 percent of the total value of $4,500 (200 shares × 22½ per share).

Nonetheless, when buying in the middle of a firmly developed trend (more on this later) or when my portfolio is heavily weighted with shares of the more conservative issues like convertible bonds or convertible preferreds, I use margin as a low-cost loan. Sometimes I don't use it at all; in other markets, I push it to the limit. In a nutshell, if good digestion and proper sleep are important to you, resist the siren call of the margin account. If you don't mind the occasional upset stomach or sleepless night that these accounts can mean in turbulent markets or volatile securities, enjoy the additional leverage a margin account can bring you.

SELLING SHORT

Short selling is nothing more than selling a security that we don't own. Can't be done, you say? Sure it can. It might be easier to think of it as selling a security that we don't own *yet*. Viewed that way, we regularly see everyday examples of selling short. If a coworker tells you that he would pay $100 for tickets to a rock concert and you don't have any tickets, you consider it a missed opportunity. But if you have a neighbor who, just this morning, told you she was sick and couldn't go to that concert and would be willing to sell *her* tickets for the face value of $40, you have an opportunity. Suppose you can't reach your neighbor but just *know* that she's home in bed sleeping and couldn't possibly have sold them, and you tell your coworker to give you the $100 and you'll deliver the tickets to him in the morning. You've just consummated a "short sale": you've sold something you didn't yet own, figuring you'd buy it, later, at a cheaper price than you sold it for.

Short selling securities works the same way. If you're convinced, for whatever reason, that a particular security is about to fall out of bed, one way to profit from this occurrence is to sell that stock short. You "sell" it at $100 per share and buy it back later for $40 per share. Your brokerage firm "lends" you the securities so it can deliver them to whoever bought them from you. Later, when you buy them back, the broker accepts the shares to pay off the "loan." (Of course, the broker has been charging you interest this whole time, and, if a dividend is paid, your account is debited and the buyer is credited the amount of the dividend). We could make this subject a lot more complicated—and most people do—but, as Henry David Thoreau said, "Simplify! Simplify!"

Do I recommend short selling? Yes—the same way I recommend margin accounts: "to everything there is a season." In firmly developed downtrends, protected with buy-stop orders, short selling can be a strategy with (mostly) controlled risk and excellent reward. Since stocks typically fall faster than they rise, there is definitely money to be made riding the "down" moves as well as the "up" moves in them. It is an essential technique with which we should be familiar in order to compete effectively. We'll discuss short-selling in greater detail in Chapter 12.

COMMODITIES FUTURES

Finally, no chapter on investment alternatives would be complete without a full and detailed listing of all the benefits of trading in commodities futures:

1.
2.
3.
4.
5.
6.
7.

OK, I know there must be *some* benefit to trading commodities. I just can't think of any. If you really want to speculate in commodities futures, this book will not help you. Charles Mackay's *Extraordinary Popular Delusions and the Madness of Crowds* or Gustave Le Bon's book *The Crowd* will be more apropos. Even better might be Freud's *Interpretation of Dreams*. Actually, I have a much better suggestion for those of you who want to speculate in commodities futures. Just write me a check instead. I'll put it to work on some of the strategies outlined in the second part of this book, make a nice, secure, respectable return of 10 to 20 percent, compounded annually, and *tell* you I'm putting it into the various commodity speculations. Then you'll have the vicarious thrill of losing all that money and, after a couple of years or so, when you've reached the pit of despair, I'll send you back all your original money, along with 5 or 10 percent interest, and I'll keep the rest of the profit I've made. Sound fair? If it does, then you *are* ready for the commodities futures market.

CHAPTER 3

CAN WE MAKE THIS A TEAM SPORT?

*Mutual Funds, Unit Investment Trusts,
and Closed-End Funds*

The short answer to the chapter title's question—"Can we make this into a team sport?"—is no. The longer answer, however, is that we can sure make it seem more like a team sport. Just as entrants in the decathlon are individual competitors, so are we, as investors, ultimately completely responsible for our own success or failure in investing. But, just as those athletes each have a "team" consisting of coaches, trainers, supportive friends, and fans, so can we enlist the aid of others in achieving our financial goals. There are many ways to assemble such a team, but one of the most common is through the use of mutual funds.

Note that I said "the *use* of mutual funds." This is an essential concept and absolutely critical to success in this endeavor. I happen to use mutual funds a great deal in my own investing. However, critical to my success is my understanding that I don't ever *give* a mutual fund my dollars. Rather, I *hire* mutual funds to manage part of my capital. This is not merely semantics, but a very important distinction—one that you must make if you are to achieve investment success. No serious participant in a decathlon would ever say to his or her support team, "Well, here I am. I'll just sit back while the rest of you make something of me." It just doesn't work that way in the real world. By the same token, you and I in our investing decathlon must have the attitude that we have retained a support team of the highest caliber in order to achieve success. If we take this approach, we are actually in a far better position than those athletes in the decathlon. Unlike them, we can choose which coaches, which trainers, and, by our choice of funds, even which type of competition we will encounter, just by deciding to hire one fund to manage part of our capital today and a different one, for a different investment environment, tomorrow.

Just what *is* a mutual fund? In its broadest definition, a *mutual fund* is a company that is organized to pool monies put up by a number of different individuals and buy and sell securities on their behalf. As evidence of your ownership, you receive shares representing your portion of the total securities held by the fund. The portion you own will determine how much income you earn in dividends and interest and how much profit you earn in terms of capital gains. Essentially, instead of investing by yourself, you pool capital with others, place it in the hands of a professional money manager, and participate in a multimillion-dollar, or in some cases multibillion-dollar, portfolio. Congratulations—you've now become a part of those "institutions" you always hear about on television news when they say, "There was heavy institutional buying (or selling) today."

THE ADVANTAGES AND DISADVANTAGES OF MUTUAL FUNDS

The advantages that ostensibly accrue to you as a mutual fund shareholder are threefold: professional management, diversification, and reduced transaction costs. Let's look at each of these three.

Professional Management

People often buy into mutual funds because the notion of "professional management" is very appealing. It's important for us to make the point, right here and now, that professional management doesn't necessarily mean *better* management. It merely means *full-time* management. In any given year, decade, or type of market, the results achieved by professional mutual fund managers, as a group, are about what you would expect from the population at large. That is to say, perhaps half of all common-stock mutual funds will outperform any broad-based average, while half will underperform. That doesn't mean that there aren't significant benefits to professional management. As a matter of fact, as we'll see shortly, certain mutual fund managers regularly outperform both the broad-based averages and what most of us could achieve on our own. Nonetheless, there is a general tendency, especially if we don't know something about a given subject, to assume that "experts" exist and that those experts will do a better job for us than we would for ourselves. This is a seductive—and wrong—notion. Nobody will watch your money as closely and care as much whether you make or lose more of it as you will. Professional management, in and of itself, is a given of mutual funds. It shouldn't be the reason you choose to invest your money. The *quality* of that professional management is what you should consider when investing in a mutual fund. All of them are "professionally" managed—some of them well-managed professionally and some of them poorly managed professionally. Just as there are good doctors and bad doctors, and good lawyers and bad lawyers, there are top-quality money managers and also-rans. Professional management in and of itself isn't the important thing. That just means that, rather than doing some other form of work, someone is getting paid to make buy and sell decisions for a living.

Diversification

Diversification is a much more tangible benefit of *all* mutual funds. True, some of them may be so overly diversified that they can never beat the market. (As a matter of fact, some funds are established with this as their charter. These funds are called *index funds*. Index funds don't try to beat the market. They simply diversify so completely by purchasing, say, every stock in the Standard & Poor's 500 that they will always do as well as the market—no better, no worse). Other funds, like the sector funds so popular nowadays, may be poorly diversified by choice. These funds invest only in a certain industry, which can make for some wild and crazy rides on the upside as well as the downside. (They still diversify, but only *within* the chosen industry.) As a general rule, the diversification offered by mutual funds is a very real benefit. If, on our own, we have only enough money to invest in, say, three securities, and just one of those companies has serious problems, we've lost up to a third of our total capital. If, heaven forbid, two of those three companies should get into serious trouble, that's two-thirds of our capital. Since one of the essential commandments of investing is, "Risk not thine original capital," the diversification offered by mutual funds provides a great cushion against this eventuality. Virtually all mutual funds invest in at least 40 or 50 different securities; most have an even more diverse portfolio.

Lower Execution Costs

The third benefit of investing in mutual funds is that, because they are large institutions, they negotiate far better commission rates than you or I would. As a result, they can often trade 100,000 shares of a stock for as little as 2 or 3 cents a share. Try asking your stockbroker for a similar rate on your 100, or even your 1,000, shares.

TYPES OF MUTUAL FUNDS

Open-End Mutual Funds

While open-end investment companies, closed-end investment companies, and unit investment trusts are all technically mutual funds, we are really referring to the open-end investment companies when we use the term "mutual fund." These are companies that do not have a fixed number of shares outstanding. Rather, they issue new shares whenever a new investor wants to purchase them and buy those shares back whenever an investor wants to redeem them. The price at which shares are bought and sold is a function of the "*net* asset value" of the fund, the number of shares outstanding, and any commissions or fees charged. Net asset value (literally, the total assets divided by the number of shares outstanding on that day) per share changes daily. There are two reasons for this: first, the total value of the securities held by the fund changes daily as the prices of the stock in its portfolio change and second, the number of shares outstanding changes daily as some shareholders redeem their shares and other individuals purchase shares.

The benefit of this open-end arrangement is that mutual fund shares are usually highly liquid, which means that they can easily be converted back into cash. You can make money three ways with any mutual fund. In the first way, the net asset value rises and you sell your shares for more than you purchased them for. In the second way, if the fund holds either debt securities or bonds or dividend-paying common stocks, you receive dividend income. In the third way, the fund sells certain of its holdings and declares a capital gain on that sale, and you receive a prorated share of those capital gains.

There are a couple of different ways you can buy mutual fund shares. One is directly from the fund itself. (This is usually done in the case of "no-load" or "low-load" funds. A no-load fund charges no initial "load," or sales charge, to purchase shares. A low-load fund charges a fee in the range of 2 to 4 percent.) The second way you purchase a mutual fund is through a salesperson, such as a commission-based financial planner, a stockbroker, an insurance agent, or, in some cases, a fund salesperson. These funds usually carry a sales charge of up to 9 percent.

Mutual funds are a massive force in the marketplace today. Not long ago, in the mid-1970s, there were only some 600 mutual funds of every stripe and color. Back then, their total assets under management were somewhere in the range of $40 billion to $50 billion. Today, there are about 3,000 mutual funds, whose assets under management total somewhere in the neighborhood of $800 billion. To put this into perspective, the total amount of savings that Americans have in savings banks and in savings and loans is about half that figure. How many of today's 3,000 funds will be around at the bottom of the next bear market? Realistically, probably not more than half to two-thirds. When the flow of investing dollars dries up, there will be only so many funds that will be able to jump up and down and wave their hands in the air, saying "Me, me, pick me." The rest of them will go the way of the great white ibis.

Closed-End Mutual Funds

Closed-end investment companies, usually called "closed-end funds" for short, typically offer their stock to the public only once. They do so via an initial public offering, just like any other common stock. Also like other common stocks, they may trade over the counter or on any of a number of exchanges, although, for the most part, they trade on the New York Stock Exchange. There are fewer than than 200 of these closed-end funds. Just like their open-end counterparts, these funds manage portfolios of stocks and bonds. The difference is, you purchase these funds as you would any other common stock. You call your broker, instruct him or her which of the funds to buy or sell, and, in many cases, get immediate confirmation. Because there are no armies of salespeople or screaming ads proclaiming their virtues, these companies often sell at a discount to their net asset value. As a matter of fact, some investment gurus often advise their clients to purchase certain closed-end funds when they are at X percent discount to the net asset value and to sell them when they approach net asset value.

Among the closed-end funds are funds for every purpose. In the discussion that follows, when we talk about selecting funds and the various types of funds, remember, it's up to you to decide whether you want to buy open-end or closed-end. Many investors have been successful with both fund types. Both are quite liquid, both give you full-time management, both offer diversification, and both transact business at reduced commission rates when they buy and sell assets within the fund. So why would the fund's management choose to be either open-end or closed-end? The real benefit to a fund's management in choosing the open-end structure is that, since the amount of money they make is usually dependent on the total assets under management, it is in their own best interest to see the fund grow as much as it can. The best way to do this is to place no upper limit on the number of mutual fund shares that can be sold and, therefore, the number of new securities that can be purchased in the marketplace and placed under management.

The benefit of a closed-end fund to its managment, in contrast, is that, once the shares have been placed in the hands of the public, the fund manager need not be concerned about redemptions. That is, while managers of closed-end funds may not be able to get new funds in as readily as their open-end counterparts, neither will they have the problem in a bad market of massive redemptions forcing them to sell securities out of their portfolio that they do not wish to sell at this point. In a closed-end fund, once the shares are in the hands of the public, they can be bought and sold among members of the public just as common stocks are, but that doesn't alter the fund's assets in the slightest.

How does all this affect you as an individual investor? Well, you can find good performance in both open-end and closed-end funds, and you can find abysmally bad performance in both open-end and closed-end funds. It all depends on what your investment objectives are and on how successfully the management of the fund, whether closed-end or open-end, load or no-load, can implement the goals that you feel are important. Along these lines, there is one caveat to bear in mind when dealing with an open-end fund. Make certain that that fund does keep some cash reserves available for possible redemptions. (When we speak of cash reserves with mutual funds, we don't mean that they actually keep cash sitting in the bank, but rather that they purchase short-term securities, usually U.S. government obligations, that can be liquidated immediately to cover any redemptions that, say, a 508-point decline on 600-million-plus shares can engender.)

For example, the Fidelity family of mutual funds is considered by many to be quite well-managed. It is also, however, one of the most aggressive. Many Fidelity funds, in the months prior to the Crash of '87, were virtually "fully invested." This means that they had only a token amount of cash or cashlike securities (government bonds, CDs, bankers' acceptances, commercial paper) against the eventuality of serious redemptions. As a result, when the markets began to panic the week ending October 16, 1987, and when there was no news over the weekend to change this growing unease, and when both the Tokyo and London Exchanges opened in the wee hours of Monday morning New York time with massive dumping of U.S. stocks, there was no place to hide. Fidelity had to sell something like a billion dollars worth of securities in order to meet customer demands for redemption. Now, when a billion pound gorilla tries to fit through a door designed for humans, the gorilla may not escape unscathed—but it's going to be very, very bad for the door.

Unit Investment Trusts

Unit investment trusts (UITs) are formed for the purpose of purchasing securities, usually bonds, which are then held in *trust* for a fixed period of time. The investor therefore obtains the benefits of diversification and, on a one-time basis, the reduced commissions that purchasing in such large quantities brings. Once these trusts are set up, however, nobody is minding the store. Once the bonds are in the account, with rare exceptions, they stay there—win, lose, or draw—until maturity. For many people who are going to purchase long bonds and hold them until maturity anyway, this is a good way of gaining diversification. For purposes of this book, however (as we'll see in Part 2, when we talk about winning strategies), active management by us is essential to our investment success. As a result, for most of us, the UITs aren't as good for us as would be an investment in an actively managed fund. There is one advantage to UITs, however: you don't pay for full-time management, because there is none. As we'll see in the next section, the internal charges levied by mutual funds can be rather substantial. They usually run between ½ and 1 percent per year but can sometimes go as high as 1½ percent or, in the case of some funds, can go to 2 percent or higher per year. Even at 1 percent, over the course of 20 years, we are looking at 20 percent levied against the value of the asset.

On a portfolio of common stock, where the manager has been averaging an 11 percent per year compounded return, that may not be so bad. Assuming that we reinvest all dividends and capital gains, this simply means that we are compounding now at 10 percent per year instead of 11 percent per year—not so great, but not bad when you consider that someone is actively watching the market and making what we presume to be well-informed decisions. In the case of bonds, however, some people prefer simply to buy quality and put it away. It isn't worth it to them to pay a management fee on top of the load they've paid to get into the fund in many cases, just so the fund manager can weed out the occasional bond that doesn't work out. If you're investing for income, and you're getting only 7 percent, that extra 1 percent charge means that you're really getting only 6 percent. Thus, some people prefer the unmanaged portfolio that they can find in the UIT. (Given the record of some bond fund managers, perhaps they're on to something!)

So why would we, as active investors, make the decision to make mutual funds part of our support team? For much the same reason that an athlete with all the ability in the world still chooses to avail himself or herself of the services of a coach. In the case of investing, it's because we recognize that, sometimes, somebody else may know something that we don't. In fact, we're willing to admit that there are better market timers than us and there are better stock pickers than us and we're willing to hire them when we find them. We said, you'll recall, that there were some 3,000 mutual funds. Of those 3,000, I personally would want to invest in 90 to 100, or 3 percent, of them. Nonetheless, I believe that these represent real value to me, or I wouldn't purchase them.

"LOADS" (SALES CHARGES)

Some market professionals claim that there's never any reason to buy a load mutual fund. I disagree. When I hire a fund to manage money for me, all I care about is the total return on those funds. If it's true that I can have exactly the same return without paying a load as I can by paying one, then I would, of course, go for the no-load. In fact, I either own or have owned load funds, low-load funds, no-load funds, and closed-end funds at various times. Many investors feel that if they can hire professional money managers of the caliber of Michael Price of Mutual Shares or Albert Nicholas of the Nicholas Fund, and pay no load, they're way ahead of the game. However, the best-performing mutual fund of the last decade has been Fidelity's Magellan Fund. The fact that it costs 3 percent initially to have Peter Lynch, the head of Magellan Fund, on their support team, is insignificant to many when the total return for that fund over the past 10 years has been in the neighborhood of 1,500 percent. Taking this a step further, I don't know of many funds or individuals that have beaten John Templeton's record over the long haul. Today, $10,000 invested in the Templeton Growth Fund in the mid-1950s is worth over $800,000. This is a gain of

8,000 percent. Take *that* to your local bank and see how the CD rate compares. Not only that, $10,000 stuffed into your mattress 30 years ago would now buy a quarter of what it did then, but, invested in the Templeton Growth Fund, it would buy 20 times as much as it did then. Yet the Templeton Growth Fund is a load fund. You'll pay up to 8½ percent for the privilege of purchasing it. Many investors obviously feel that if you can make 8,000 percent on your money, even after paying 8½ percent, you'd be pretty silly not to. They're still happy to take 7,992 percent over that period of time! Finally, we can also hire quite a bit of talent for our support team by purchasing closed-end funds. Again, many will take the market savvy of a Warren Buffet in Berkshire Hathaway or a Charles Allmon in the Growth Stock Outlook Trust any day.

So what's the bottom line? When investing in a mutual fund, you do it on the basis of the long-term track record of the fund, its investment goals, and your decision on how successfully you believe the fund has diversified and how clever and agile the fund's management is. Of course, we must remember that all funds charge yearly expense fees based on assets under management as well. Therefore, all other things being equal (though they seldom are), a no-load fund held for any length of time that performs exactly the same as a low-load or load fund is better. That is to say, *given equal performance,* a no-load is better than a low-load is better than a load, and a no-load without a "12b-1" clause is considerably better than one with it.

Because of 12b-1 fees (so named for the SEC regulation that allows them), the distinctions are blurring between what constitutes a load and what doesn't. In addition to the low-loads that we've already discussed, and in addition to the fact that each individual mutual fund charges a different series of fees to manage the portfolio, and in addition to the exit fees (also called redemption fees) that some funds now charge, there are 12b-1 fees, which pay for the marketing and advertising costs that the fund incurs as well as (sometimes) trailing commissions to brokers. It's up to the fund to decide what constitutes a marketing cost. The problem is that they tend to add up. For instance, if you are deciding between two funds and you believe that both will achieve exactly the same results over the same period of time, you could choose the one with a front-end load of 8½ percent or the one that is no-load but levies a 1 percent annual 12b-1 fee. If you then wanted to redeem your $10,000 investment on which you had gotten, say, a 12 percent annual return year in and year out, here's what would happen: At the end of the first year, the fund you paid the front-end load of 8½ percent on could be redeemed for $10,248. The fund that invested your $10,000 without a load but with a 1 percent annual 12b-1 fee would be redeemable now for $11,088—an advantage. The same thing happens for the first few years. At the end of the fifth year, for instance, the 8½ percent front-end load fund would have returned to you, at 12 percent annual return, $16,125. The no-load fund with the 12b-1 fees would have returned $16,651. If, however, you keep either fund for any significant length of time, there is a subtle shift in terms of which returns the most to you. At the end of the 10 years, the front-end-load fund would return you $28,419. The supposedly no-load 12b-1 fund would return $28,394. At the end of 20 years, the fund that you paid an 8½ percent load charge on would return $88,264, whereas the "no-load" fund would return $80,623—nearly $8,000 less.

INVESTMENT GOALS OF MUTUAL FUNDS

While a mutual fund can take only three general investment approaches—to seek growth of capital or to seek income and preservation of capital, or some combination of the two—the ways in which various mutual funds get there are many and varied. Reading the fund's prospectus will allow you to identify it's investment goals, risks, and various fees, charges and expenses. *Always* read the prospectus provided by open-end funds. We noted earlier that there are currently some 3,000 different mutual funds. That proliferation might be explainable if there were 2,000 or 3,000 different mutual fund companies. There aren't. While there are a number of different companies, a great deal of the assets under fund management in this country are invested with a handful of huge mutual fund companies that offer every conceivable type of mutual fund in order to attract every investing dollar. It's safe to say that probably between two-thirds and three-quarters of all dollars invested are invested with mutual funds that are part of a fund family—that is, with two or more different funds with different objectives managed by the same company. Probably the largest of them all is Fidelity. The last time I looked, Fidelity had around 100 different funds. Other large fund families include Value Line, Scudder, Alliance Capital, the Colonial Funds, Eaton Vance, MFS, the Seligman Group, T. Rowe Price, Kemper, Vanguard Group, Putnam, IDS, American Funds, Dreyfus, the Franklin Group, and the American Capital Group. Within each of these fund families and, indeed, among the many other fund families and individual funds, we can find mutual funds of every size and description. Some small funds have less than $1 million in net assets, while Fidelity's Magellan Fund has something like $8 *billion* (8,000 times more). The smaller funds, especially in their early years, can often take sizeable positions in a few securities, which may allow them to have extremely good (or extremely poor) performance depending on how well a few individual issues do. Once a fund gets to be the size of a Magellan, however, there's no way that one individual security can make a significant difference. For that reason, many advisors tell people they should stick with the smaller funds. You can't argue with success, though. Even though its most rapid growth occurred in the earlier years, the Magellan Fund has averaged a compounded return of something like 30 percent for the last 12 years. That far exceeds the performance of virtually every other mutual fund, large or small.

Large or small, old or new, fund family or individual fund, we still have to decide whether we want to invest primarily for income, growth, or a combination of the two.

Income Funds

If we choose to invest for income, a number of types of *income funds* are available to us. For instance, we can purchase equity-income funds. These portfolios emphasize the high-dividend-paying stocks and high-dividend-paying preferreds and convertible bonds, though they may also purchase some corporate bonds. If we'd rather not assume even the minimal market-volatility risk of these kinds of equity-income funds, we could instead go for the high-yield corporate bond funds and have a different kind of risk, the risk of interest rate fluctuation. These funds invest largely in *junk bonds,* a term not of derision (well, not normally anyway) but of rating-service fact. A bond is considered a junk bond because it is rated less than investment grade by the two primary rating services, Moody's and Standard & Poor's. Probably, sooner or later, some of these bonds will default. Therefore, many investors who want to receive the higher yield they offer invest in them through a high-yield mutual fund. If 3 percent of these bonds default in any given year (which sounds about right), but the percentage paid in interest on them is 4 to 5 points higher than those of investment-grade bonds (also about right), then it is worthwhile to many people to own them.

A third alternative is those high-grade corporate bonds. A number of mutual funds purchase only investment-grade corporate bonds. These funds may actually outperform the higher-yielding "junk" portfolios if the economy goes into a tailspin, because, even in a severe recession, these bonds are not nearly as likely to default as are the bonds issued by companies of lesser quality.

Another category of income mutual funds consists of those which specialize in U.S. government bond funds. These portfolios are heavily weighted with bonds issued by the U.S. government or its agencies, like GNMA, FNMA, and FHA. Actually, as a subset of this group, there are mutual funds wholly devoted to GNMAs, or Ginnie Maes, which are securities issued by an agency of the federal government that purchases mortgages from banks (it is theoretically possible for you to inadvertently purchase a piece of a Ginnie Mae in which your own mortgage resides); these pay not only interest but a portion of principal each month.

Another type of income-oriented mutual fund is the option income fund. These funds write options on the securities they hold in order to smooth out the fluctuations in their net asset value and to increase the yields. This sounds good in practice; in fact, the performance of these funds has been so-so. Then there are the "target funds," which buy bonds that all mature in the same year. The idea here is to give investors who are willing to keep their funds in the fund for a fixed term a predictable stream of income and a clear sense of what the investment will be worth on a given date. This is helpful for investors who want the diversification of bonds and want the professional management of a fund but know they'll need to take the cash out for some specific purpose, like funding their child's college education 15 years down the road. Also included in the area of income funds are all those municipal bond funds, which can themselves be broken into the high-yield (junk) muni funds, the high-grade muni funds, and the single-state muni funds (which invest only in the issues of a particular state). These funds are of benefit to individuals living in states that have a high rate of personal income tax. In all the above cases, investors can find funds that invest for the short term, the intermediate term, or the long term.

We should also list under income funds the various money market funds, both those secured by corporate obligations and those secured by government obligations, and finally the tax-free money market funds. These are technically mutual funds, even though their investment objectives are merely to preserve capital and to stay current with or just slightly ahead of inflation by investing in short-term instruments, with maturities ranging from one day to 30 days or so.

Growth Funds

If you are one of those investors who, when you see the dividend and interest checks coming in, respond with, "That's nice," but are more interested in a *real* return on your money—something on the order of 15 or 20 or 25 percent—then you will probably be more interested in *growth funds*. Since most of the returns generated by growth funds are generated by buying and selling individual stocks, as the securities held by the fund increase in value, your fund's share price will reflect these changes and you'll benefit. Growth funds fall into two primary categories: those which consider themselves *long-term growth funds,* whose purpose is to steadily increase share value, year on year, and those which consider themselves *maximum-capital-gains funds,* which are willing to assume a greater risk in terms of either market timing or stock selection in pursuit of what they hope will be greater profits.

All growth funds carry varying degrees of risk. In general, the risk in any growth fund comes primarily from the volatility of the underlying shares. For this reason, growth funds are usually considered riskier than income funds. No matter how brilliant the management team and no matter how well diversified the portfolio, when the bear starts snarling and stocks enter a protracted decline, most growth funds will suffer. Of course, when the bear goes back into hibernation and the market turns bullish, these funds rise in concert with the underlying market. Or, as John F. Kennedy once observed, "A rising tide lifts all boats." (John Kenneth Galbraith may have one-upped him, speaking about the stock market, when he said, "Genius is a rising market.")

The stocks chosen by fund managers of the maximum-capital-gains funds are the ones that are more sensitive to market movements. Therefore, these funds are the ones that are hardest hit in declining markets and usually outperform the longer-term growth funds in skyrocketing bull markets. One variation on the theme of long-term growth funds is the aforementioned index funds. Index funds, recognizing that most mutual funds fall short of average performance, don't even try to beat the market. Instead, the index fund will create a portfolio based entirely on a broad-based market index, usually something like Standard & Poor's 500 Index. Using an index fund, you as an investor will have a greater responsibility to yourself to make market timing decisions. Yet you'll know, when you see what "the market" did on any given day, that your mutual-fund portfolio did pretty much the same.

Another type of growth or maximum-capital-gains fund is the specialized fund: sector funds, precious-metal funds, international funds, and global funds. Let's take these in reverse order, if only because it will clear up right away the distinction between global funds and international funds.

Global funds invest globally. International funds invest internationally. There, aren't you glad we cleared that up? Actually, global funds invest anywhere on this globe they want, including the United States as well as foreign countries. As a result, these funds end up with a portfolio that is very widely diversified because it is spread not only among different securities but also among different economies. If you'd like to dip your toe into the market for foreign stocks, investing in a global fund is a great way to start.

International funds, in contrast, invest anywhere in the world that they want *except* the United States. As a result, these funds would usually be purchased by someone who already has positions in U.S. stocks or who feels that the U.S. market represents the poorest opportunity for gains at a particular time. A relatively new subset of the international funds are those which invest only in the affairs of a single country or a certain region of the world. Single-country funds abound. There are single-country funds for Canada, Mexico, Italy, the U.K., Germany, Japan, Korea, Taiwan, and Malaysia, to name just a few. In addition, a number of regional funds specialize in securities of the Pacific Basin or Europe or even smaller regions such as the Scandinavian countries as a group. In the last couple of years some fund families have even begun to offer shares in securities that the fund families believe are destined to be the blue chips of what they call "emerging markets"—those less developed countries which are about to enter into that phase of their national history where they will be enjoying the admittedly mixed benefits of industrialization, globalization, and mass communication and transportation.

Precious-metal funds primarily own shares of gold and silver mining companies. There are precious-metal funds that specialize in other precious metals and defense-necessary metals, in addition to those which own mostly gold or silver bullion. Precious-metal funds usually do very well in times of high inflation (or when the expectation exists in the minds of most investors that there *will be* high inflation.) Within this category, you can find mutual funds that further specialize geographically. For example, some funds invest exclusively in South African mines. Since South Africa is far and away the world's largest producer of gold, with a number of companies in that country dedicated to this pursuit, you would expect to find a number of these companies in many mutual funds. The purest play is probably ASA International Limited, a closed-end fund trading on the New York Stock Exchange. Given the political hazards in South Africa and given that many investors have decided not to support a totalitarian regime even indirectly, it's not surprising that a number of other mutual fund companies have been established that invest exclusively or primarily in North American or Australian mining stocks. Remember that the volatility of precious-metal funds is extremely high. During periods of high inflation or investor uncertainty, these funds can reward you with sizeable returns. Of course, Sir Isaac Newton would be very disappointed if I didn't remind you that what goes up sooner or later does come down again. The stock market is subject to the physical laws of motion as well. During periods of low and declining inflation or when investors feel very good about the prospects for industrial and service companies, gold stocks do not merely languish, but often lead the decline.

The arguments made in favor of *sector funds,* the last group of specialized funds that we'll look at in the growth area, are seductive indeed. If you're willing to take larger than normal risks, you can get larger than normal rewards—sometimes. Sector funds, of which there are more than 100 already and which are multiplying fast, buy shares of companies in one particular industry. As a result, at any given time, since there is very little diversification in sector funds, one of them will almost certainly be the hottest-performing mutual fund of all. Of course, almost by definition, one of them will always be the worst, as well. The rest of them will line up somewhere in between. In bull markets, the top few sector funds will most likely return more than the average equity fund. Of course, the few worst-performing will always do worse. What makes sector funds an easy sale is that it allows us to choose the industry we feel most strongly about. That way, we can fool ourselves into believing that all we need full-time management for is to pick and then monitor a portfolio of stocks that are the best within the industry we have chosen. If I sound somewhat skeptical about sector funds, that's because I am. The whole idea of investing in a mutual fund is that I have chosen to hire certain money managers to diversify my portfolio. If I have chosen my money managers well, then I've left it in their hands to diversify. If I've made the active decision that they can diversify, but only within the industry that I've chosen, why did I bother to invest with them at all?

Something between ½ and ⅝ of the success we will achieve in investing can be attributed to the movement of the market itself. Another ¼ to ⅜ is directly attributable to the performance of the individual industry. That leaves only ⅛ or at most ¼ attributable to factors like management, cash flow, earnings per share, and all the other occasionally useful information on the individual company. Since so much of the success of our investment depends on being in the right market and in the right industry, I'd rather select fund managers wisely and then let them move from industry to industry as they see fit. In sector funds, the manager concentrates on stocks within only one industry. The advantage of sector funds is that they allow us to *attempt* (please note the emphasis) to time the market better. For example, during the early stages of an economic recovery after a recession, we might want to choose financial-services stocks or utility stocks, which profit when interest rates are low. As the recovery progresses in the underlying economy, we might want to switch to consumer and leisure-sector funds. At the point at which the economic recovery is mature, we might want to switch to heavy-industry stocks and cyclicals.

If you are convinced that a major secular trend was going on, you could benefit from using sector funds. For example, you might purchase utilities-sector funds if you believe that utilities are significantly undervalued vis-à-vis other stocks and will appreciate over the course of a few years. or you may believe that, as most Americans grow older, stocks in the medical, drug, and health-care industries will enjoy tremendous success. Purchasing for the long pull and dollar-cost averaging (which we'll talk about in Part 2), you might benefit in these two situations by using sector funds.

Total-Return Funds

Our last category of mutual funds consists of those funds which seek to provide both growth and income. These are listed as either "growth and income" or "total-return" funds. *Total-return funds* seek to combine the relative safety and the higher income of government and/or corporate bonds and high-yielding common stocks with the growth potential of growth-type stocks. The objective is, therefore, steady long-term returns with greater safety and less volatility along the road.

Total-return funds have always been attractive for most investors, but there's an even more important benefit today. The recent tax "simplification" and "reform" (which may have rearranged, but certainly didn't simplify!), by removing the distinction between capital gains and ordinary income, made total-return funds, which usually offer a good income stream, more attractive.

There are two general types of total-return funds. The first, *balanced funds,* usually try to balance their investing between bonds and stocks. For the most part, they try to get the growth part of their return from the stocks they choose and the income part of their return from the bonds they choose. In an effort to mollify potential investors who might be concerned that their money manager will get caught up in the euphoria of the day, many of the balanced funds will write into their prospectus that they will always keep a certain percentage of the portfolio invested in bonds.

The second type of total-return fund, *growth and income funds,* invest more in high-dividend-paying stocks like utilities, established financial-services concerns, and the big, well-established manufacturing companies, as well as in convertible bonds or convertible preferred stocks. As you might expect, total-return funds tend to dampen or absorb the shocks of skyrocketing and plummeting markets. They will usually underperform the maximum-capital-gains funds in an up market, but will significantly outperform them in a down market. Over an extended period of time, many total-return funds do every bit as well as, and in some cases even better than their growth or maximum-capital-gains counterparts.

Regardless of the type of mutual funds in which you choose to invest, you still have the onerous task of narrowing it down from 3,000 potential choices to the very few that you'd like to hire to manage some of your money. How do you do this? There are a number of periodicals that regularly review the mutual-fund industry. Among the best of these are *Forbes, Money Maga-*

zine, Consumer Reports, and *Changing Times.* Of all these, I find *Forbes* the most helpful, followed by *Consumer Reports. Forbes* is perhaps the most exhaustive tabulation, and its often-trenchant prose puts the numbers in perspective. *Forbes* also publishes, as part of its annual mutual fund survey, its "honor roll" of mutual funds that have consistently done well in good times and bad.

What I particularly like about *Consumer Reports'* rating of mutual funds is that it doesn't assume a one-time fixed invest-ment of, say, $10,000 in a fund in a certain year and then estimate how well it would have done X number of years in a row. Rather, they ask, "What would have been the results of investing in a certain fund with fixed dollar amounts every year?" That is, *Consumer Reports,* realizing that most of us have to put money into our investments as we earn that money, assumes that we put in, say, $2,000 per year for five years and then measures what the effect would have been with only that amount of capital at any given time.

Now that we know everything that we need to know about the types of funds, about classifying funds on the basis of their objectives, and about where to get information on the funds, all that remains is to find out where and how to buy them. The reports *Forbes* and the other publications mentioned above will include the toll-free numbers that you can call to request a prospectus and new-account information for each of the funds they discuss.

SCHWAB'S MUTUAL FUND MARKETPLACE

There is yet another way of investing in no-load and low-load funds besides going directly to the mutual-fund company. There are some brokerage firms that offer a centralized marketplace for a number of no-load and low-load funds. The firm I work for, Charles Schwab and Company, offers such a service through the Schwab Mutual Fund Marketplace. What Schwab does is allow you to purchase any of more than 300 no-load and low-load mutual funds from many of the large families of funds we dis-cussed earlier as well as a number of individual funds. Schwab has growth funds, income funds, total-return funds, and every combination and permutation within each of these. Remember, these funds are not managed by Schwab but are the same funds you would purchase if you called the fund directly. The difference is that, rather than having to open a new account and fill out a new-account application every time you want to switch from one fund to the next or having to get your signature guaranteed by a banker or broker every time you want to sell, you simply pick up the phone and tell Schwab what you want to do. Schwab pools your orders with those of other investors and then executes them with each individual mutual fund through the Schwab omnibus accounts it has with those funds. These mutual funds can also be purchased on margin, should you choose to seek the extra leverage (and the extra risk!).

Why would someone purchase a no-load fund, which they could purchase for no fee directly from the fund, through Schwab or some similar service that charges a transaction fee? The answer is—convenience. Many investors who purchase mutual funds that they are going to hold for a number of years purchase them directly from the funds themselves. But investors for whom there is even a chance that they will want to sell quickly or swap for another fund do so through the Schwab Mutual Fund Marketplace because when they want out, they want out. They don't want to have their signature guaranteed, they don't want to send letters, and they don't want to wait a day or a week. That kind of convenience and security, on thousands of dollars of investments, in their minds is well worth the transaction fee.

We started this chapter with the question, "Can we make this a team sport?" The answer is still no. Investing, like competing in any sport that pits one individual against another, remains a solitary activity in which your success is always most important to you and you alone. And you have the right and the responsibility to yourself to hire the best help you can in the form of various coaches and trainers. An investor who hires successful money managers who have a proven track record is just like an athlete who enlists the assistance of coaches and trainers who have demonstrated their ability to help other athletes succeed. Doing this in your investing can make you a winner, too.

CHAPTER 4

CAN WE READ UP ON
THE GAMES?

*The Financial Press, Full Disclosure,
and Other Myths*

When competing in the long-distance running events of the decathlon, you can run with the crowd for awhile in order to pace yourself, but if you expect to win the race, you must eventually pull away from the crowd. The same is true in investing: as long as you run with the crowd, you are an also-ran. By definition, "the crowd" is where most of the competitors are. As any statistician worth his or her salt will tell you, that's called regression to the mean. For our purposes, the mean means—mediocrity. In investing, as in competitive running in the decathlon, it may be more comfortable to stick with the crowd (at least you don't feel lonely); but, whether running in the decathlon or investing, we are not in it for the company. We are in it for the rewards. Bear this analogy in mind when pursuing your own investment goals. When you find yourself running with the pack, you should feel claustrophobic rather than comfortable. Running with the pack, *by definition,* means you'll never win.

I am essentially contrarian in my approach to making money in the market. I get distinctly *un*comfortable when I find that my friends, my fellow professionals, *The Wall Street Journal,* and "Wall Street Week" all think the same way I do about the market's direction and velocity. This doesn't mean that we need to be contrary for the sake of being contrary; it's not that we *are* contrary, it's that we *act* contrary to the mainstream of investment thinking. The only way to find out what that investment thinking is, is to tune yourself in to the financial press. Can we read up on the games? We not only can but *must,* in order to pull ahead of the pack. Just bear in mind, as we survey the various publications and other information sources available to us, that we do not read the financial press to learn what stocks "the experts" tell us we should purchase and then purchase them, nor to find out where "the experts" tell us the market is going and then act accordingly. Quite the contrary, we read and listen in order to take the pulse of how fast and in what direction the pack, as represented by these supposed experts, is running.

The experts most often quoted on the television news programs devoted to business and in the financial press are people who have something to do with *other* people's money. Every now and then, one of the networks or magazines interviews a very successful individual investor. I often listen carefully to what these successful individuals have to say, then ask myself, "Does what this person has just said make sense? Has he or she looked at all the possibilities? Has he or she considered what can go wrong with his or her scenario?" I do the same thing when I listen to or read an interview with a respected expert who is charged with a fiduciary responsibility or who has a particular ax to grind in selling securities to the public. The difference is, such experts usually control tens or hundreds of millions of dollars or more. By the time they express their opinion as to the direction of the market, in 99.99 percent of the cases they've already acted upon their own advice. Now they are looking for the comfort that comes from having other people follow their lead.

Does it make sense that these people would, before committing their own funds, advise the rest of us on the virtues of their communications? I have yet to see the experts say, "The rest of you go ahead and act on this. As it unfolds successfully, then I'll jump in, paying a higher price." No, in virtually every case the course they are espousing is the one they've already taken. Again, if every single expert you hear on television or read in the newspapers or financial magazines is telling you that "the market has nowhere to go but up" or that "we are in a new era of investing" or that "there are no sellers," then I will wager you in any currency you care to name that they've already acted on their own advice. Now, if absolutely *everyone* is telling you to buy and if 99.99 percent of them have already bought, then answer me this: Who is left to buy? The answer, in all too many cases, is just you and me and the other poor lost souls who have, once again, done their part to demonstrate the validity of the greater-fool theory by being the very last ones to buy before the inevitable decline begins. That's not to say that I don't find ideas for purchases that I would not have been exposed to if I hadn't read the financial press. It does mean that the fact that someone else likes a particular stock is not a compelling reason in and of itself for *me* to like it. All the expert has done is save me the time and trouble of unearthing the opportunity myself. This is the point at which many people turn off their minds and blindly follow the advice of the expert recommending a particular issue. *This is precisely the time your mind must turn on, not off.* With these caveats in mind, let's take a look at the various media available to us in what we generically call the financial press.

DAILY SOURCES OF INFORMATION

The Wall Street Journal

The single best source for daily business and stock market news is still *The Wall Street Journal*. The *Journal* has run a series of television and print ads in which it claims to be "the daily diary of the American dream." Well, depending upon what stocks you own, the *Journal* may also be the daily diary of the American nightmare. But, whether your own holdings are dreams or nightmares, very few come close to giving the kind of complete coverage that the *Journal* does. You can get business and financial highlights in your local newspaper; you can look at the business section of *The New York Times,* arguably the best metropolitan newspaper for business reportage; you can purchase *Investors Daily,* a fine newcomer which has better technical data, clearer "sentiment" analysis and stock charts *The Wall Street Journal* would do well to emulate. As a matter of fact, when we discuss timing our entry into or out of the market, in Chapter 13, you'll see that some critical yardsticks I recommend are found only in *Investor's Daily.* For these reasons, I personally read both papers. As a business person and an investor, I find the *Journal* most helpful. Were I only reading for investment information, *Investor's Daily* would be my choice. Let's take a look at the *Journal* first.

I find something of interest on almost every page of *The Wall Street Journal*. I get news summaries of important national and international affairs (albeit not as timely as the stories in the local newspaper), reports on national and international business and finance, and regular, thought-provoking features and articles on people, places, and events that make a difference in this world. I also get great editorials and art, theater, movie, and book reviews and light human-interest stories, and, not least, I get virtually every piece of information I need to make informed decisions on the direction of the market, its velocity, and which investments I want to be in.

The *Journal* comes in three sections. The first section covers the most important business, national and international news of the day. It also covers politics (on the back page of the first section), economic news, on page A2, and, often, gives special coverage to a particular industry or company.

The second section is targeted primarily at the business person. Titled "Marketplace," it contains articles about competing, marketing, and managing. It deals with industries and companies, enterprise and technology, marketing, media and the law. Perhaps most importantly, it also deals with personal careers, career planning and management techniques, successes and failures.

Finally, the third section, "Money and Investing," deals with, well, money and investing. It's here you'll find solid information on all the financial markets, personal finance stories, the various stock tables and information on the stock, bond and mutual funds markets.

I find most of what I need to make my investment decisions in the third section of the *Journal*. Actually, I read the paper from back to front. I find the statistics, graphs, and economic and market data to be accurate and easy to understand. I also find the opinions expressed in interviews with famous experts on the second page of section 3 of the *Journal* (in the "Abreast of the Market" and the "Heard on the Street" columns) to be mostly *inaccurate* and easy to understand. These are the first two columns I turn to when reading the *Journal*. I can depend on the *Journal* to quote the kind of experts that I discussed earlier—those mainline analysts, trust officers, and economists who collectively control hundreds of billions of dollars. If I find that, day after day, all those being interviewed in these two columns, especially the "Abreast of the Market" column, tell me what a great market we're in—that "the old yardsticks don't apply anymore," that "we needn't worry even though the market is historically higher" in terms of price-earnings ratios or any other indicator of an overheated market—then I know that it's time to begin lightening up. *They just told me in no uncertain terms that they are already fully invested and see no reason I shouldn't be, too.* In that environment, I have to begin questioning, if they are already fully invested, *who is left to buy?* If, however, day after day, I read interviews with all these respected movers and shakers wherein they proclaim that there are no buyers left, that the state of the nation or the world or the universe is such that stocks may never recover, or that it's the worst market that they've seen in their lifetime, then it is time for me to start nibbling. Again, if they all think it's so bad that none of them are buying (and if the world isn't coming to an end), sooner or later some of them will say, "Gee, this thing looks awfully cheap. Maybe we should do something with those hundreds of billions that we are sitting on." Earlier, I talked about that billion pound gorilla trying to get out the door. When all these people decide they want back in the market, that's a few hundred billion pounds of gorilla trying to get *in* the door. Thank you very much, I would like to be already through the door rather than fighting them for entry.

The "Heard on the Street" column does for individual industries and issues what the "Abreast of the Market" column does for the market itself. That is, I find great opportunity after an industry has been panned two or three or four times in the "Heard on the Street" column. Using the same logic as I do for the market in general, seeing an industry or company thrashed regularly in this column gives me my "buy" signal. By the same token, of course, when an industry or issue has been hailed as the best thing since somebody thought up the idea of a publicly held company, that's my "sell" signal.

Most of the time, we don't see these blanket statements to the effect that "It's a new era! The market's going to the moon!" or the "It's the end of Western civilization. The market will never come back." What we usually see is all kinds of waffling, doubletalk, hedging, and in general the kind of conversation that leaves us scratching our heads and saying, "What did they really *say?*" When we reach those two extremes and we do see these extreme kinds of quotes, that's when we are most likely to be within just a few months of an absolute market bottom or an absolute market top. I don't try to play every little hiccup in the stock market. Specialists, member firms, marketmakers, and floor traders can't do it consistently, and they spend their entire lives literally on the floor of the exchanges. Only liars and leprechauns can hope to catch all the myriad bounces, hiccups, and gyrations within the primary trend. By positioning yourself in the most uncomfortable position, however, you will find that you are right more often than wrong. You recall we said that the less comfortable you feel about diverging from the consensus, the more likely it is that you are beginning to run away from the pack and win the race.

It's also in this section that you'll find great graphs, charts and statistical data which give you a snapshot of the marketplace. For instance, prominently displayed on the first page of this section are charts depicting the Dow Jones Industrial Average, an indication of where interest rates are headed (based on the Federal Funds rate), an idea of what bonds are doing (based on the Shearson Lehman Treasury Bond Index), a chart of where the U.S. dollar has been (based on the Morgan Guaranty Index versus fifteen currencies) and a sense of what's going on in the commodities arena. Below these charts is a section titled "Investment Insight" which presents a different viewpoint on some facet of investing each day. Back on page 2 of this section, you will also find the stock market "Data Bank" for that day. This shows the action in the major indexes: the Dow Jones Industrials, Transportations, Utilities, and composite; the New York Stock Exchange indicators, the Standard & Poor's Indexes (including the S & P 500 and its constituent components—the 400 industrials, 20 transportations, 40 utilities, and 40 financials); the NASDAQ (National Association of Securities Dealers

Automated Quotation system), Indexes of the over-the-counter (OTC) composites, which consist in turn of the OTC industrials, the OTC insurance companies, the OTC banking issues, and two indexes of the most popularly traded over-the-counter securities, those comprising the "national market" securities and their composite averages and the averages of just the industrials; and, finally, in the "Others" category, the American Exchange Index, the Value Line Index (a broader-based index of securities), and the Wilshire 5000 and the Russell 2000 (two very broad-based market indicators).

Also in this section are those issues which have traded most actively on the New York Stock Exchange, the over-the-counter market (listed under NASDAQ), and the American Exchange. There is also information on the number of issues traded, those which advanced, those which declined, the number that made new highs and new lows, what the advancing, declining, and total volume was, and the number of block trades (those trades executed in blocks of 10,000 shares or more by institutional investors). Here, too, we will find the stocks that were the highest percentage gainers and losers and the volume percentage gainers, as well as half-hourly trading figures in New York Stock Exchange stocks.

I'll let you discover for yourself the editorial page and the rest of what makes the *Journal* a great newspaper. Again, as an investor who's also a business person, if I had to choose only one source of information regarding the stock market, this would be it.

Fortunately, I don't have to choose only one, so I also read *Investor's Daily*. *Investor's Daily* is laid out more like a modern newspaper (as opposed to the *Journal's* columnar format in its first section). *Investor's Daily* also has considerably better charts on companies and industries than does the *Journal* and has some information that I find essential which is nowhere to be found in the *Journal,* such as the "Psychological Market Indicators" found on *Investor's Daily's* "General Market Indicators" page.

What should you do? Read a copy of both newspapers and decide for yourself. Either way, you can't go wrong.

The Financial News Network (FNN)

There is one other source of daily information that I find occasionally helpful (and always lots of fun): the Financial News Network, or FNN, which is available to cable subscribers in most parts of the country. (If you don't have FNN, you may have an FNN clone in the form of a local station that devotes itself to stock market commentary, thinly disguised advertising, and not-so-thinly disguised advertising.) FNN is a hoot. I love it. I find some of its programming and advertising addictive in the same way I find a carnival sideshow addictive. FNN has responsible financial journalists interviewing some of the most respected names in the business. As a result, I often watch in order to detect that emerging consensus that signals a primary bottom or a primary top. When, hour after hour and day after day, a never-ending stream of experts tells me to toss out all the old rules of investing because this market is so great that the old rules just don't apply anymore, I know it's time to begin entering my sell orders.

What makes FNN so much fun, however, is the quality of its advertisers. I mean, here we have some very capable interviewers and commentators interviewing some very savvy professionals, and to pay for it all they sell advertising to some of the most slipshod, fly-by-night, slick-talking, separating-you-from-your-money boys this side of the midway. That's not to say they don't also have responsible advertisers as well, but they're not nearly as much fun.

I should point out that I don't find these slick operators, who are obviously trying to sell me something, nearly as good a "reverse indicator" as the mainstream financial analysts and money managers. When I'm trying to find that major top or major bottom, I want to act contrary to the people who have the hundreds of billions behind them to put their money where their mouths are. Most of the operators who stage these fake interviews, which are blatant advertisements dressed up as "investment news" programs, simply hire someone with a good speaking voice and sincere listening expression to interview them. The thing is, they just don't have the wherewithal to be real players. If I were to act contrary to what they are saying merely because they're all in agreement, it wouldn't do me much good. Besides, these people are mostly followers. They are in business to make money. They don't make money by bucking the trend; they make money by following the trend. Given that most investors are most interested in buying what almost everybody else wants most of the time, these folks would be very poor businesspersons if they didn't offer it to them. William X. Scheinmann was acutely aware of this when, almost 20 years ago, he wrote a great little book about the market entitled *Why Most Investors Are Mostly Wrong Most of the Time*. What I *do* find is that, when all "the experts" tell me to do something *and* all the trend followers who are selling a particular product to the public line up at the same time on the same side of the market, then I know we are perilously close to a major reversal.

Remember, if virtually every respected economist and financial expert on Wall Street assures you that, say, the dollar has nowhere to go but down against the other currencies of the world and if on FNN all kinds of commodities brokers and purveyors of commodities options have assured you, always with sincerity and sometimes with logic, that you should be placing all your money at this very moment in commodities futures on the Japanese yen, the West German Deutschemark, and the British pound, you should suspect that sometime in the not-too-distant future the U.S. dollar will stage a major secular rally vis-à-vis these other currencies. Regardless of the current hot button, a democratic political system combined with a capitalist economy is still one of the niftiest ideas to come along in the last few millennia. Many would (and have) bet that the country will go through inevitable periods of contraction when the naysayers will tell us that the world is coming to an end. I won't bet that the country is going down the tubes. Besides, if the country is going down the tubes, *no* investment will work out, so it's a pretty silly and moot point.

Watch FNN. It's fun and that is, after all, one of our goals. Like our decathlon counterparts, we're doing this to win; but, like them, if we can't have fun along the way, why compete at all? This investing stuff is great, rip-roaring fun.

It wasn't that long ago that I began to amass a net worth sizeable enough to inspire me, for tax planning, retirement planning, and estate planning, to hire a financial planner. The first one I chose came highly recommended by a number of my associates. He was and is a Very Famous Planner. He'd written a couple of books, published regular articles in a number of publications, and spent far more time on the lecture circuit getting new customers than he ever did thinking about financial planning for people like me. All in all, he had all the trappings of an expert, including the fact that he was deadly dull. This gentleman pointed out to me, early in our professional relationship, that there was nothing fun about investing. "The husbanding of one's resources," he intoned, "is a very serious matter." I fired him shortly thereafter and hired a financial planner who is eclectic and fun-loving and smart. As I said, I'm in this to win *and* to have fun along the way.

WEEKLY SOURCES OF INFORMATION

Barron's

If you can't have the fun of providing yourself with daily market fixes, then you may want to avail yourself of one of the weekly or less frequent periodicals, newspapers, or television shows that will still keep you in tune with the stock market. If you can devote time to your portfolio only, say, once a week, the best thing for you to do is to purchase *Barron's* every single week. If you thought my recitation of all the information you can find in *The Wall Street Journal* and *Investor's Daily* was exhausting, wait till you see *Barron's*. The "Market Laboratory" provided by *Barron's* is probably the most thorough compendium of statistical information on the market. If you have time to read only one publication per week, make it *Barron's*. In the same two or three hours that you would spend reading the funnies and the ads from your local department store in a regular newspaper, you can get a complete blow-by-blow recap of all market activity for the week as well as every—and I mean *every*—piece of statistical information about each and every market in our investing decathlon and any number of others as well. *Barron's* features lengthy articles with noted experts as to the course, direction, and velocity of the market, industries within the marketplace, and individual issues. *Barron's* also provides the trenchant and witty commentary of Alan Abelson, its managing editor. Abelson can deflate any expert's balloon, rain on anybody's parade, and still have enough energy left to discredit charlatans of every persuasion. As a matter of fact, the only shortcoming I find in *Barron's* is that it comes out only once a week. I want my market news on a more frequent basis. In all other respects, *Barron's* is absolutely superb.

"Wall Street Week"

One other source of weekly information that I find extremely worthwhile and helpful is "Wall Street Week," the weekly half-hour television show produced by the Maryland Center for Public Broadcasting and featuring the worldly-wise and wise-of-word Lou Rukeyser. There is much to enjoy in this show. Besides Lou's penchant for powerhouse punning (and that in itself is reason enough to watch!), this show does a number of things well. It is a serious attempt to assist investors, no matter what their means, in assessing the news of the week and making investment decisions based on that news. Lou's tongue-in-cheek humor lightens the delivery without trivializing the message. Right after the weekly update of what stocks did, there is a very helpful segment for lazy market observers. This feature is the Technical Market Index. Basically, this index consists of a number of indicators, which may or may not line up with one another to give a clue as to market direction. Virtually all these indicators are what are sometimes called "sentiment" indicators, which means that they attempt to gauge investor psychology. Well, you know this will get my attention, because it's something I can use as a contrary opinion indicator. Among the items measured in the index are the level of insider trading activity, which documents whether corporate officers and directors are buying or selling stock in their own company. Another is a measure of the put-call ratio, or how many investors are buying puts and how many are buying calls. Another measures the percentages of investment-newsletter writers who are bullish and bearish. Almost all the items in this index are contrary opinion indicators. This is one of those cases where somebody else has already done some of my homework for me. The staff technicians who prepare the Wall Street Week Index have already pored through the pages of the *Journal* and *Barron's* and saved me the time. I never mind when someone else wants to compile the data; I just don't let them do my thinking for me.

Normally, you'll see fluctuations within the Wall Street Week Index somewhere from a range of minus 5, which is a very bearish signal, to plus 5, which is a very bullish signal. Bear in mind, however, that this indicator is not always right on. For instance, during the Crash of '87, the Wall Street Week Index was no help whatsoever. Nonetheless, the truly lazy investor could do worse than simply buy stocks—or, better yet, a broad-based basket of stocks such as we would find in a growth mutual fund—whenever the Wall Street Week Index reaches plus 5. Hold that position until the Wall Street Week Index falls to minus 5. You won't catch every move this way; you may occasionally get whipsawed; and you won't have the fun of staying in tune with the market on a more frequent basis. But you will do better following this simple indicator than you would by buying blind or by listening to the experts. (Of course, now that I've said this, somebody will fiddle with the index and change the components or, over time, the index's validity will decline and someone *won't* fiddle with it, and the thing will be worthless. But for now, it's a great timing tool.)

The other benefit of "Wall Street Week" is that *only* certified, dyed-in-the-wool, establishment-type experts get on the show. While Lou Rukeyser has a healthy skepticism about the pronouncements from on high made by these worthy souls, apparently most of those watching the program do not. Stocks touted on "Wall Street Week" usually go up in the week following the broadcast, only to come right back down in the weeks and months that follow, usually much more severely than they went up. Again, a very healthy contrary opinion opportunity is provided by "Wall Street Week." I try not to miss it.

MAGAZINES AND NEWSLETTERS

Magazines

You may find a number of other publications helpful. None of these will give you the breadth and depth that those mentioned above will, but some of them are very good nonetheless. My personal favorite of this group is *Forbes*. *Forbes,* while it has excellent reportage on industries, companies, and the movers and shakers within the business world, is really more for those of us who take our investing very seriously. *Fortune* and *Business Week,* its two primary rivals, focus more on the business aspect and less on the investing aspect. There are a number of others, like *Money* and *Financial World,* that dedicate themselves to the investing side, but if I could choose only one of the lot, it would be *Forbes*. Malcolm Forbes's irrepressible enthusiasm for the free-market system and the free exchange of ideas comes through on every page. This is another publication I often read from cover to cover. The columnists in *Forbes* are nonpareil. Like them or dislike them, agree with them or disagree with them, I find them almost universally thought-provoking. If I have only a limited amount of time, I'll look here first. Later, when I can enjoy it, I often read the rest of the magazine.

Forbes publishes some articles I can do without—like its annual "400 Richest People in America" issue. In many cases, these people are simple not interesting enough to justify all that verbiage. It seems, upon reading even one of these issues, that there are three primary roads to wealth in America today: be born with the right set of parents and, through no cleverness, uniqueness, or facility of your own, outlive them; deal off the bottom of the deck or shortweight people often enough so that you can place what you steal from them in your own bank account and later buy respectability with it; and (at last!) perceive a need, find a unique way of filling it, and doggedly pursue it your entire life. This last group I find fascinating, the first two groups boring at best. For the most part, however, every issue of *Forbes* is great. And the one *Forbes* issue that I never miss is the annual mutual-fund survey, which we talked about in Chapter

3. The quality of the research is matched only by the quality of the reporting in this issue. My only hope is that if Malcolm Forbes ever decides to go off into the sunset aboard his well-stocked yacht, he has trained his sons to carry on with the tradition of skepticism and evenhanded reporting that is the hallmark of *Forbes*.

Investment Newsletters

Finally, there are hundreds and hundreds of investment newsletters you can purchase. The best newsletter about investment newsletters is the *Hulbert Financial Digest,* published by Mark Hulbert. In this publication, you will find your favorite newsletters held up to the light of reality—a harsh light, indeed, for many of them. Hulbert tracks the successes and failures of these newsletters by monitoring their recommendations. Many of them are regularly hoisted upon their own petard. This is a case of "You can run, but you can't hide." No matter how flowery their ad copy, no matter how out-of-context they quote themselves in their direct-mail solicitations, Hulbert keeps them honest.

There are financial newsletters for mutual fund investors, options traders, commodities traders, market timers, single-industry investors, and hundreds more. The best way to get an idea of the diversity of publications available is to visit your public library. If you live in a large community that has a business library, so much the better. In a decent big-city business library, you'll probably find between 50 and 150 investment newsletters. Take a look at them—better yet, a long look. Take a notepad and spend the day. Start reading the various publications and, whenever you find one willing to make a flat statement, write it down. Then go on to the next one and write down its projections. What you'll probably find is that for every five newsletter writers who tell you something is black, five others, looking at the exact same indicators, will tell you that it's white, and 300 others will tell you that it's a really a shade of gray. (After the fact, of course, they'll tell you they knew all along which way it would go.) If you subscribe to too many investment newsletters or, indeed, if you listen to too many of these analysts on television or radio, you will end up thoroughly confused and incapable of taking action.

My recommendation, therefore, is to find two or three publications you really enjoy, and stick with them. That doesn't mean you need to take their advice and follow it blindly. I've taken trial subscriptions to dozens of investment newsletters, but I find that, for my particular circumstances, I get pretty much what I want from two publications. That's not to say that others aren't equally good or that I might not benefit from subscribing to them, as well. *You'll want to reach your own conclusions,* but I have found that *Professional Investor,* written by Robert Gross, and *Personal Finance,* edited by Richard Band, give *me* just about everything I want. Bob Gross is a market technician and a very fine one. I'm not. I'd rather let someone like Bob read the tea leaves of the market and summarize his technical findings for me biweekly in his newsletter and more frequently via his telephone hot line. Bob devotes two pages to his market commentary and gives over the rest of the newsletter to any recommendations he may have for common stocks and warrants, mutual fund switching strategies, options, PRIMEs and SCOREs, and gold stocks. He also devotes a page to the current market stance of some of the more respected advisory letters that he competes with. Finally, there's a whole page devoted to the various technical indicators, too numerous to mention here but including things like the advance-decline ratio, trend lines over or under their 30-week moving average, odd-lot short sales, insider buying, mutual fund liquidity, the short interest ratio, member shorting, bellwether stock action, weekly high-low differential, and many, many others.

I believe that understanding investor psychology is the most important component of stock market success, and many of these indicators measure just that. You'll often hear people disparage technical analysis (and often with good reason!). But there's a big difference between, on the one hand, trying to read into an individual stock chart a "head and shoulder formation," an "island," a "saucer," a "flag," a "wedge," and all the other paraphernalia that chartists honestly believe they see and, on the other hand, looking at those sweeping indicators which give me a sense of what most people have really done with their money. Technical analysis of *major* secular trends is essential.

The other thing I like about *Professional Investor* is that Bob Gross is acutely aware of the all-too-human frailties of others as well as of himself. He makes no claims to infallibility, as lesser writers do, and in fact is scathingly honest about his own investment successes and failures. Given a choice, always go for the one advisor who is too hard on himself than for 100 that are too easy on themselves. Too many investment advisory services pursue the path they have touted long after the logic for doing so is bankrupt (as are many of their clients), simply because they are unwilling to admit they were wrong. While this may salve their egos, it destroys your bank balance.*

Another publication that I find quite helpful is *Personal Finance*. Its editor, Richard Band, is a kindred contrarian. As a matter of fact, he has written an excellent book on the subject, titled, appropriately enough, *Contrary Investing: The Insiders' Guide to Buying Low and Selling High*. I don't always agree with Richard Band, any more than I always agree with Bob Gross. Also, *Personal Finance* runs numerous articles about rare coins, insurance as an investment, and various commodities tactics. I don't happen to include any of these "events" in my investing decathlon. Nonetheless, I still read these articles in order to see if there is any compelling reason for me to reconsider them and also because I do occasionally learn something in these articles that helps me in my own decathlon. Like Bob Gross, Band provides a telephone hot line that is updated weekly and deals primarily with the securities in *PF's* model portfolio.

I find that Band, like Gross, is very honest about his failures as well as his successes. *Personal Finance,* like *Professional Investor,* is not afraid to take a stand, but neither is it afraid to reverse directions when the weight of the evidence has shifted. *PF's* "Capsule Advisory" always gives, in the briefest of formats, a great overview of a number of important issues. The questions

---

*Tough as it is to find good technicians who remember and learn from their mistakes, South Floridians are fortunate to have two such pros within a few miles of each other, Bob Gross and Stan Weinstein. Stan Weinstein, the author of *Stan Weinstein's Secrets for Profiting in Bull and Bear Markets,* is also the editor of another fine newsletter, *The Professional Tape Reader.* Since I recommend that you find coaches and trainers that you feel comfortable with, you might take out a trial subscription to both *Professional Investor* and *the Professional Tape Reader* and see if either meets your needs.

and answers often carried on the back page are also quite helpful, as is the "Market Watch" section on the front page, which outlines in just a few paragraphs the editor's opinions on the directions of the primary markets.

In short, the technical information in *Professional Investor,* the fundamental information in *Personal Finance,* and the unparalleled information regarding investor psychology that I find in both fulfills most of my information needs.

BOOKS ON INVESTMENT

I have found a number of books very helpful in my own investing decathlon. Rather than review them here, I've listed them under "Suggested Reading" at the back of this book, which you may want to take a look at now. Some of the ones I've found helpful relate directly to the stock market, but many more deal with "the human comedy." In the investment decathlon, understanding what makes people follow the crowd and how they behave when they do so is far more valuable than understanding the difference between current assets and book value and the net present value of future earnings.

OTHER SOURCES OF INFORMATION

There are three other sources of information regarding industries and individual companies that I will briefly discuss. Only one of these is considered to be a component of the financial press: stockbrokerage firms' research department recommendations. The two others are corporate financial reports and new-issue prospectuses. Most of them are on the up and up, but because the information is so easy to manipulate, I don't rely on them.

Stockbrokerage Firm's Research Recommendations

Let's deal first with stockbrokerage firms' research recommendations. The bottom line is: I don't trust them.

Years ago, I started out in this business as a retail stock-broker with one of the top two or three investment banking firms in the country. This firm published reams and reams of research material, each report duller than the one before it. Since my sales manager reminded me daily that I was there to sell and the research department was there to research, I tried honestly to rely on the recommendations the firm gave me. Thank God, for the sake of my clients, that I caught on rather quickly that this was not the way to make money for them.

Listen, competitors, common sense will tell you that there is an inherent and inescapable conflict of interest in brokerage firm research. Do you honestly believe an investment banking firm that tells you, even if it believes it, that you should sell shares of a company's stock, when you know that the firm's income depends on the managers of that company choosing the firm to handle its next major offering? It certainly isn't a slight against management if the time is right to sell. Maybe the entire industry is topping out or maybe the entire market is topping out. Maybe there are things beyond the control of company management and, while we believe they will get their arms around the problem, it will take a couple of years. There may be much better opportunities than this stock. Yet, if the investment banking firm's research department tells you you should sell that stock now, the senior officers of the company, whose net worth is tied up in stock options and executive perks related to that company, are not going to be happy. If they're not happy, then the next time a financing opportunity comes along, you can bet your bottom dollar they're not going to use the investment banker that told the public to sell their stocks, because they will conclude (inaccurately, by the way) that that advice drove the price of their stock down.

It's an incestuous relationship from the beginning and, no matter how loudly the stockbrokerage firm may proclaim to you that it (and it alone) keeps the investment banking side of the house strictly separate from the research side, don't believe it. So what's the benefit in brokerage firm research reports? Well, like many of the experts we've discussed before, these folks can help us determine the best time to buy or sell. If virtually every brokerage firm on the street is touting a particular issue, you can bet that, inside of a few weeks, every full-commission stock-broker in America will be told by their managers that they should advise their clients to buy this stock. Investors will receive research report after research report in the mailbox. Even those investors who don't receive that firm's brokerage research will read about the fact that everyone in the world is recommending such and such a stock in the "Abreast of the Market" section of *The Wall Street Journal,* in *Barron's,* on FNN, and so on. The net result is that when everybody believes so strongly in something, and everyone puts his or her money behind that belief, there comes a time when no one is left to buy. When that happens, and the first timid soul says, "Excuse me. I have to sell 100 shares," no one remains who wants to buy the stock who hasn't already done so. Such is the stuff of which market tops are made.

Corporate Financial Reports

The next area to discuss is corporate financial reports—both annual reports and the various interim reports. Any self-respecting annual report contains three elements: pictures, words to accompany those pictures, and figures that usually have nothing to do with the words or pictures. For the most part, if the company has done well the annual report is a chance to gloat, and if they've done poorly it's a chance to rationalize. (A notable exception is the annual reports from the redoubtable Warren Buffett, CEO of Berkshire Hathaway. It's worth owning the stock just to get Buffett's annual reports.) My suggestion is that you doodle on the pictures and, if you read the prose at all, read it with a very jaundiced eye.

That leaves the numbers. While I believe that most companies make every effort to report honestly on their progress for the year and their true financial condition, a hundred judgment calls can be made in accounting for various items. You'd better believe that the management team of any publicly traded company will, in most cases, choose that method of accounting which places their company in the most favorable light in the eyes of the shareholders. After all, life in corporate America, with all its executive perks, can be downright comfy. Sure, it isn't as good as being a basketball player or a rock star or a politician, but pretty cushy, nonetheless. As a result, beware of taking at face value any numbers you read in an annual report.

There are some basic things in annual reports that you want to look at. One is the *income statement,* which tells you how the company did in the current year compared to the previous year. Then there's the *balance sheet,* which purports to tell you the company's financial condition—that is, what it owns and what it owes. And, third, there are footnotes. These are the most fun to read. As a general rule, if your time is limited, always read the information in the smallest print first. This is the information that, in many cases, company management must put in because the various regulators force them to, but they don't really want you to read. By definition, that's where all the dirt is. And that's also where all the good stuff is.

If you are really interested, there are numerous books and publications that will teach you how to read financial reports. As to whatever you read in these reports, let me just say that, in the balance sheet, management can play around with the accounts receivable, the allowance for doubtful accounts, the inventories, the prepaid expenses, the fixed assets, the depreciation, the intangibles, the accounts payable, the notes payable, and the accrued expenses payable. In short, depending on how you want to record the numbers (and that is one of management's jobs), there's a lot of opportunity for "give and take." Traditionally, about the only item not subject to interpretation on the balance sheet is "cash." (Of course, in these days of foreign currency arbitrage and such, even that may soon be questioned.)

The same is true of the income statement. Net sales, cost of goods sold, depreciation and amortization, and selling, general, and administrative expenses can be different from quarter to quarter, depending on how the company chooses to report them.

New-Issue Prospectuses

Finally, we should mention something about prospectuses. Too many investors believe that, since initial public offerings have to be registered with the Securities and Exchange Commission and since the SEC was established, at least in part, to protect the investing public, then the SEC has somehow condoned the information contained within the prospectus. *Nothing could be further from the truth.* If you read the cover of any prospectus, you'll find the same words: "These securities have not been approved or disapproved by the Securities and Exchange Commission nor has the Commission passed upon the accuracy or adequacy of this prospectus. Any representation to the contrary is a criminal offense." Forewarned is forearmed, and let the buyer beware! But still, day after day, people buy initial public offerings, somehow assuming that they've been blessed by the SEC. A prospectus is nothing more than a disclosure document. It may not always be full disclosure, any more than an annual report, another disclosure document, is a full and complete picture of the company. There are also many differences that we encounter when reading a prospectus. Let me give you two examples.

The following is a direct quote from the initial public offering prospectus of the Charles Schwab Corporation:

> The focus of Charles Schwab and Company, Inc., has been, and will continue to be, on serving the needs of independent investors by providing high-quality, low-cost brokerage and other financial services. I believe that as financial information and education become more widely distributed, more individuals will conclude that they can do a better job of meeting their financial needs if they take personal control of their investment decisions. Based on this belief that the number of independent investors will continue to grow, our company will continue to invest in expanding the range of our products and services, increasing the size and capabilities of our branch network and computer systems, and improving the quality of our service to our customers.

I'm biased here. Chuck Schwab is my boss, and I happen to agree with his vision and the strategy that follows from it. But whether you share his vision or not, his statement gives a very straightforward explanation to potential investors of what his philosophy is in running his company. It's up to each individual investor to weigh all the facts and all the risk considerations in deciding whether he will be successful in meeting this goal. At least his goals and strategies are right there before you.

Now let's look at a different prospectus. I am indebted to the *Growth Stock Outlook,* written by Charles Allmon, for reprinting this little gem:

> This offering is of securities of a startup company with no operating history and no plan of operation; the company will not engage in any business whatever until after the completion of this offering. . . . The company does not know what business it will engage in and has no plan of operation. . . ."

I could go on, but I think you get the message. Here's a company organized for no purpose other than to take your money so that the people behind it can spend your money rather than their own while they decide what they want to do when they grow up. And people bought it.

A prospectus is no protection against a company that has absolutely no idea what it will do with the money it raises from you, the greater fool. I once, as a lark, invested in one of these companies, because a friend of mine in the brokerage industry knew the principals. I purchased 3,000 shares at 16 cents each in a company that had no ongoing business but was going to "acquire other businesses" and add the value of management expertise. My friend believed strongly in the track record of the principals, and, upon researching it, I did have to agree that they were pretty savvy players. The bottom line? The stock went from 16 cents to 2 cents in the three months after it was offered, and it never did recover. Yes, they did acquire a couple of companies. I believe they now have an ice cream franchise and a biotechnology company. Synergy at work.

As you can see, an awful lot of information is available. You could read 24 hours a day and still not absorb all of it. For the most part, the published information that's available is considerably better than the supposed "inside information" that your broker, bookie, or erstwhile best friend give you. The information is all there—most investors simply don't see it. If you stick with the suggestions made in this chapter—pay close attention to what the experts are saying and separate yourself from the pack when they are all running together, watch the technical, fundamental, and psychological indicators readily available, and look at some of the publications that I've suggested for background information—you should do well. Be chary of investment advice from brokerage firms, company financial reports, and new-issue prospectuses. And remember, none of the publications we've listed absolve you of responsibility for making your own decisions. Let them do some of the homework—then *you* decide if it's been done well or not. Only by doing this successfully will you distance yourself from the pack and cross the finish line first.

CHAPTER 5

WHO HIRED THESE COACHES?

---

*Stockbrokers, Financial Planners,
and Investment Counselors*

No track and field athlete simply wanders onto the field one day and, without coaching or previous training, breaks world records. Of course, many amateur athletes have tremendous natural abilities and, with no one to assist them in developing those abilities, still do passingly well. But to scale the heights of world-class competition, even the most gifted athlete needs coaches who can study and improve upon their technique and trainers who can carry out the plan of action that will make them winners.

Likewise, to succeed in the investment arena, we need at least some assistance. That assistance takes a number of forms. It consists of reading up on the rules and techniques of the game, seeing how others have succeeded, doing a few dry runs, and hiring one or more of the inhabitants of this chapter—stockbrokers, financial planners, and investment counselors. If you're new to the game, don't merely chart your progress on paper. Rather, take some Monopoly money or some other form of play money in the exact amount that you would be investing in the market. Then, when you make your decision to purchase a security, take that amount of play money and actually put it in an envelope marked on the outside with the number of shares and the name of the security you have "bought." Seal the envelope as a reminder that you can't get this money back any more than you could once you had instructed a stockbroker to purchase it for you. Invest this way for six months to a year. That won't be enough time to experience primary trends going in both directions, but it will give you an idea of just how fickle the market can be. It will also force you to begin studying the stock quotations you see in *The Wall Street Journal* and will give you a strong sense of the finality of the decisions you make. Assuming that you play the rules (and since you are the winner or loser in either case, you may as well play by your own rules), this method will give you a feel for the excitement and the potential rewards and pitfalls involved in making investment decisions. When you make the decision to sell a security, then, and only then, unseal the envelope and take the money out and put it back in your "account" envelope. At the end of the six months to a year, take out the money, close out all positions and see where you stand. If you've come out ahead, try to determine why. Were you lucky? Did some investments work out better than others? Why? By the same token, if you've lost a great deal, tear up the money and flush it down the toilet. Ask yourself why you lost and amend your investment strategy accordingly. Better you should lose with play money than with real money. If your experience is typical of most others, you'll find that it is quite easy to lose 100 percent of your capital in options and penny stocks, for instance. If you are honest with yourself, you can learn a great deal by the time you start playing with real money. Even then, it might be a good idea to modify this procedure only slightly—that is, when you're hearing that little voice inside of you that says, "Go for it, you can do it! Take the 100-to-1 shot," actually put all that cash in real dollars into an envelope and GIVE it to your brokerage firm. This will bring home to you just how risky the course of action you are about to embark on is. Think of all the things that cash could have bought at your local audio-video store, sports shop, clothing store, or auto dealership.

Let's suppose you've done this and now it's time to play with real money. Just how do you go about doing so? You are going to need a stockbroker, or at least a stockbrokerage firm. That's not to say that you can't purchase securities directly from friends, relatives, and coworkers, but they can provide you with only a limited universe of securities to buy and sell. The whole idea of purchasing securities listed on an exchange or over the counter is so that you can purchase whichever ones you choose to at any given time. And to do that, you need a middleman—a stockbrokerage firm. Whether you choose to do business with an individual stockbroker or a stockbrokerage firm that does not assign you an individual stockbroker is entirely up to you. You may or may not choose to seek the assistance of a financial planner, and you may or may not choose to have someone else assist you in managing your money, like one of the major investment counseling firms. Let's talk about stockbrokers first.

STOCKBROKERAGE FIRMS

There are some basic decisions that you need to make when choosing a stockbrokerage firm. The first of these is, do you want to invest through a full-commission brokerage firm or a discount firm? I can't answer that question for you, and neither can anyone else. It depends on your level of investing sophistication, your willingness to take the time necessary to follow the market and your individual securities, and your comfort level with your own—and others'—decisions. If you are the kind of person who doesn't yet have a great deal of investment sophistication, the only honest answer is that neither type of broker is really for you. You should select a mutual fund or funds as discussed in Chapter 3 until you're comfortable with your decisions. Remember, there are pros out there who will eat you alive. This particular arena, unlike the decathlon, is no place for amateurs.

How about the amount of time you have to invest? Or, more appropriately, the amount of time you want to spend researching your investments and monitoring them after you've entered into them? If you have limited time, or if you are the sort of person who would rather trust someone else's judgment than your own, you are probably better off with a full-commission brokerage firm. But if you are willing to seek your own investment ideas and to devote the time needed to monitor your investments, *and* if you believe that your decisions are every bit as good as a stockbroker's, then a discount brokerage firm is probably the best place for you. As the name implies, a discount brokerage firm can save you substantial amounts on commissions.

Full-Commission Firms

If you choose to do business with a full-commission brokerage firm, you have some choices to make. Do you choose one of those big, established national brokerage firms that spend so much money on image advertising during the World Series and the Super Bowl? Or do you feel more comfortable at a regional brokerage firm, which may also be a member of the New York Stock Exchange but which deals primarily in one geographic area of the country? And do you choose the brokerage firm, or do you choose the individual stockbroker? That is, does it really matter which firm the stockbroker is with as long as you have a good relationship with him or her? The answer is, your first time out the results will probably be about the same whichever way you go. The idea is to make certain that the brokerage firm you choose is a member of the principal listed securities exchanges.

The New York Stock Exchange is far and away the biggest and most prestigious of the lot. Since there are hundreds of New York Stock Exchange "member firms," it should be relatively easy to find one in your community. Being admitted to the New York Stock Exchange means that (1) the brokerage firm can afford to buy a seat on that exchange, (2) it has agreed to abide by all the exchange's rules and regulations, and (3) it wants to be thought of as a major player. Biggest doesn't always mean best in the stockbrokerage business. Besides, with all the hype, it's tough to tell who really is the biggest. Right now, of course, it's Merrill Lynch, Pierce, Fenner & Smith, or is it Shearson Lehman Hutton American Express, or is it somebody else? For our purposes, let's just make up the mythical brokerage firm of Merrily Sheared Mutton and use it as an example of a national brokerage firm.

When you deal with a major national brokerage firm like Merrily Sheared, you are dealing with an organization that has hundreds of branch offices and many thousands of salespersons. By the way, there's nothing derisive about the term "salesperson" when discussing full-commission brokerage firms. Stockbrokers are salespeople. Their job, just like that of a clothing salesperson, an automobile salesperson, or a real-estate salesperson, is to match products with buyers. This can work in your favor, or it can work against you; but in and of itself, it is merely a given, not a value judgment.

Perhaps the advertising of the brokerage firm is what pulled you into one of their offices to begin with—bulls wandering around china shops, the entire world coming to a standstill when they overhear who someone else's broker is, and famous actors who look like your rich uncle. If so, then you will want to simply seek out that brokerage firm's local office. You can worry about choosing a stockbroker after you've visited the office. I would not use this method of selecting a stockbrokerage firm, though, because I would like to know a little more about the company and the person that I'm doing business with. Nonetheless, it is one method. The primary disadvantage of this method is that, when you do walk in, you'll be given to "the broker of the day." The broker of the day might be an experienced broker who genuinely has the interests of his or her clients at heart and is also uncannily good at selecting securities and timing the market. This isn't a very likely scenario, however. The broker of the day may or may not be a good stock selector, may or may not be a good market timer, may or may not give a hoot about your investment success, and may or may not have any real experience in the business. Asking the branch manager to take the time to sit with you and discuss your investment portfolio and investing needs and then asking for a recommendation as to which of the brokers in the branch would be best for you to work with may not be much better. It's just as likely that the manager will be thinking, "Let's see—who do I owe a favor to that I can help today?"

The other way to choose a full-commission brokerage firm is to choose the stockbroker first and then, assuming that you also approve of the firm for which he or she works, open an account with that firm. How do you find a stockbroker? Ask your friends who invest. But don't just ask them, "What broker do you do business with?" Have some specific questions in mind. For instance, what are your friends' investing goals? Even if their broker does well by them, if their goals are completely different from your own, you are likely to be less than satisifed with the same broker. Also, you need to determine if your friends have done business with that broker for any length of time. If, in fact, they've never been through a bear market with that broker, they may be singing his or her eulogy rather than praises at some point in their investing career. You might want to try to determine the broker's experience level and any investing biases he or she has, to see if they either match or challenge your own. If you like the answers you get, then it's worth setting up an interview with the stockbroker. Remember, you are not walking into his or her office saying, "Here's my wallet. Please don't hurt me." *You are in charge.* You are hiring an investment professional to assist you in your investing decisions. This, of course, should be the same approach you take when hiring a lawyer, a financial planner, or any other business professional. If you start with this attitude and keep the relationship professional, believe me, you'll be much better off in the end. From this point on, it's up to you and whatever chemistry exists between you and the broker.

Discount Firms

Since 1975, there has been an alternative to full-commission brokerage firms. It's only fair that I state my biases here: when I entered this business, in the Dark Ages before 1975, all brokerage firms charged precisely the same commission for a given number of shares of a security at a given price. It was only after 1975 that the Securities and Exchange Commission mandated that brokerage firms would be allowed to negotiate commissions with their customers. What this has meant to the individual investor is that, instead of a great deal of disparity in commissions from firm to firm, there are now two primary groups: full-commission firms and discount firms. Shortly after discount firms came into being, I joined what was destined to be the largest such firm in the country. I am, therefore, obviously a believer in the concept.

What do you get from a discount brokerage firm? Lower commissions, sometimes substantially lower. In order to purchase the same number of securities at a full-commission firm, you would have to pay two to three times more than if you were dealing with a discount broker. Dealing with a discount firm, I avoid the potential conflict that may arise when a stockbroker calls me to attempt to sell me the individual stocks that the sales manager is, for whatever reason, putting greater emphasis on that day. Since I am not tied to any one broker, as I would be with a full-commission firm, I also like the convenience. That is, when I call my discount broker, I don't have to wait for Joe Smith, my personal stockbroker, to get back from lunch or to finish a conference with a client who is more important to him than I am. To the discount brokerage firm, my call is just as important as any other. And I don't have to wait to talk to a specific broker—anyone at that firm can help me.

What do you give up by dealing with a discount brokerage firm? In some cases, you give up dealing with a single stockbroker (though some discount firms will assign a broker or team of brokers to assist you). You also usually give up access to the brokerage firm's research and you give up the advice of that individual broker. (Depending on the quality of that advice, these may be benefits or they may be disadvantages.)

In addition, you may or may not give up certain services and products when you deal with a discount broker. Some discount brokerage firms, like Schwab, offer credit cards, debit cards, asset-management accounts, IRA accounts, Keogh accounts, certificates of deposit, lines of credit, stock-option-exercise financing, and in-house mutual funds, and can direct you to various insurance products. Check out any firm before you decide to open your account to make sure they can meet your investing needs.

Electronic Investing

Some brokerage firms also offer their clients the opportunity to place orders via their personal computer without ever having to visit or telephone the broker. Some firms also either provide quotes via FM signal to a proprietary device that they rent to you or provide both quotes and order entry via touch-tone telephones. I am most familiar with Schwab's offerings in this area: the Schwab Equalizer software is the most popular of all PC-based order-entry and information-retrieval packages and one that even the computer novice can enjoy using.

There are two guidebooks I've seen for those who are interested in reviewing all the alternatives in this type of investing approach: *The Dow Jones–Irwin Guide to Investing with Investment Software* and *The Dow Jones–Irwin Investor's Guide to Online Data Bases.*

Bucket Shops

Regardless of whether you choose to do business with a full-commission or discount brokerage firm, the one type of firm that you do *not* want to get mixed up with is a "bucket shop" (also called a "boiler room"—colorful terminology in this investing business). Some firms, particularly when they are just starting out, choose to conduct their business via a toll-free 800 number. This, in and of itself, should not be enough to scare you away from the firm, but, since there are so many bucket shops that deal exclusively from an 800 number, it should send up a warning flag that you need to proceed with at least a modicum of common sense. In other words, you should check out this firm more stringently. One simple way to do so is to ask, when a salesperson calls you with "the investment opportunity of a lifetime," for an appointment to visit them in person. If they respond that you may visit them at their offices whenever you are in their community and seek to set up an appointment with you, you may feel considerably better about doing business with that firm than if they say, "We haven't got time for a visit. If you don't act right now, you'll lose the chance to become truly wealthy."

The SEC, the Commodities Futures Trading Commission (CFTC), and the various self-regulatory organizations like the New York Stock Exchange, American Stock Exchange, Pacific Coast Stock Exchange, and National Association of Securities Dealers (NASD), cannot possibly keep up with all the fly-by-night bucket shops and boiler rooms in this country. If it's true that there's a sucker born every minute, then, since each one of these operations needs only a few suckers to make a great deal of money, then maybe there's a new boiler room opened every day. As soon as the enforcement arms of the various federal, state, and exchange regulators stamp one out, another one arises from the muck. As a matter of fact, when the principals of these organizations are finally brought to justice, most of the salespeople simply slip out the back door and go to work for other such operations.

These operators are slime. That's not an investment they are offering, it's a one-way ticket to losing all your money. You might as well simply save yourself a step and write a check to the next stranger who dials your number by accident. Remember, investments are like streetcars (well, at least like streetcars *used* to be back in the days when they ran on time). If you miss this one, wait 25 minutes or so—another one will be along. If you are telephoned by someone who asks you to part with your hard-earned money for "the last chance to become wealthy," I suggest that you, as a matter of policy, tell them, "Thanks, but no thanks."

The bottom line is that, regardless of how frequently you trade or what securities you trade, you will need a brokerage firm to provide you with the liquidity you need in order to purchase and sell securities. You may also choose to hire a financial planner or, particularly if you have a great deal of money to invest, an investment counseling firm—or both.

FINANCIAL PLANNERS

Financial planners, as the name implies, help you to plan your finances. That is, they assist you in projecting revenue and expenses connected with your job as well as any investments you have. They also assist you in tax planning in order to maximize the amount of capital you have available for investment (remember—it ain't what you earn, it's what you keep) and help you evaluate various types of investments to find a fit for your income, cash flow, expenses, and personality. So, basically, they can help you with financial, tax, investment, retirement, and estate planning. Financial planners, while they may be registered with the various exchanges in order to purchase or sell securities they have recommended to you, are not stockbrokers with a fancy name. Financial planners offer a broad range of services and usually become licensed with the various exchanges in order that, when they do recommend something that must be purchased or sold on one of the exchanges or in over-the-counter markets, they can earn commissions, as well as their basic fees, for so doing.

There are "fee-based," "fee-and-commission," and "commission only" financial planners. "Fee-based" planners charge you a fixed fee to assist you in your financial planning and derive no other income from your investment decisions. Because of this, they usually charge the most of all financial planners. "Fee-and-commission-based" planners may charge you a fee and also receive a commission if you purchase a product they recommend. There is a potential conflict of interest here, but it's no different from the conflict a surgeon experiences when recommending surgery or when a lawyer recommends that he or she represent you in negotiation. Any reputable financial planner will advise you of this in advance. "Commission-based" financial planners claim to charge you no fee for their services but, since their entire income is therefore dependent on the products they recommend for your purchase, they are likely to be somewhat more adamant (read: pushy) in their choice of investments for you. They may recommend investments that may not be suitable for you but provide a larger commission to them.

You may or may not need financial-planning assistance. If you do, I recommend that you choose a fee-based or fee-and-commission-based financial planner. I do *not* recommend that you entrust a stock-brokerage firm whose brokers are on commission to do your financial planning for you. In most cases, this is less a service than a treasure hunt for the brokerage firm. In most cases, the brokerage firm's representative or the written documentation that you get from the brokerage firm will speak grandly of prudent investments, the investing pyramid, life-cycle investing, ensuring that all personal needs are taken care of, making certain that you have enough insurance, and so on, before recommending securities. But I guarantee that no matter what your situation, there will be a recommendation that you participate in the market. After all, that's what the brokerage firm is in business for. If nobody is betting, who needs the dealer?

There are no guarantees that you will find a good financial

planner on your own. There are at least two organizations which have evolved from being merely trade associations to being education and certification bodies. The Institute of Certified Financial Planners (ICFP) requires continuing education of its members, requires that they pass a series of national examinations to determine competency, and will give referrals from among its membership. The International Association of Financial Planning (IAFP) also has continuing-education requirements and will also provide referrals. While your attorney or accountant can refer you to financial planners, I think the best way to find a good one is to ask others if they use the services of a financial planner and, if so, whether they are pleased with them. Even if your immediate peers don't use a financial planner, your boss or other persons you know who have greater income or greater net worth will do so. They'll be flattered that you asked them.

INVESTMENT COUNSELORS

Finally, if you have a great deal of money to invest, you will have your pick of a number of investment counseling firms. Some of these firms will manage as little as $50,000, while many of them will not accept accounts of less than $500,000 or $1 million. Can you achieve superior results by letting a professional manage your money? It depends. Many of the same benefits we discussed in our chapter on mutual funds apply here as well. In essence, when you pay an investment counseler's fee, you are purchasing full-time management and the diversification that you can achieve by having a substantial amount of money at work and by having a counselor who surveys a number of different investment opportunities. If you have no time for studying the psychology of the marketplace or have no patience with it or simply cannot bring yourself to disagree with the prevailing trends, then an investment counselor may be for you. Many of us, try as we may, just don't feel comfortable going against the crowd. If you find yourself in this category, and you have enough investable funds to avail yourself of the services of an investment counselor, you may want to consider doing so. Of course, you should also consider using a mutual fund to achieve the same ends. As a matter of fact, many of the mutual fund companies have investment counseling subsidiaries. Many of the same people who make the primary decisions on how to spend hundreds of millions of dollars in each of the mutual funds also manage individual portfolios for wealthy individuals and institutions.

Again, the single best way to find a reputable investment counseling firm is to ask friends, coworkers, and others whether they have availed themselves of any particular investment counselor and, if so, what their experiences have been.

The stockbrokerage firms, the financial planners, and the investment counselors—that's about it for your coaches. There's another group, though, that has a great deal to say about whether you win or lose *and* how you play the game. For a closeup view of them, let's move on to those who officiate in the arena.

CHAPTER 6

___

REFEREES, UMPIRES, AND WATCHDOGS

___

The SEC, NYSE, NASD, FRB, etc.

When we were children, most of us ran and jumped and threw things with reckless abandon and with no interest in the rules of the game. Indeed, we often made up the rules as we went along—and changed them whenever it suited our fancy. In many ways, that's how the securities markets worked during their early years as well. As a matter of fact, it wasn't until the heady 1920s, when so many new companies were brought public with stock priced to sell at greed times infinity and sold on promises, hot air, hyperbole, and outright lies, that the era of securities regulations in which we now operate began.

Nowadays, in the securities markets, just as in the decathlon, there are strict rules that must be adhered to, bodies that develop these rules, and officials whose role it is to determine whether or not the rules are being followed. In discussing all these different rulemaking organizations, we refer primarily to the Securities and Exchange Commission when we talk about federal securities regulation. There are other federal agencies charged with regulating commodities securities and the like, but the SEC sets the tone for all of them and is, at least currently, the agency charged with the broadest range of powers over the securities industry.

We commented earlier that there are a number of state securities regulators as well. Most of these design their policies according to the framework established by the SEC. For our purposes, it is worthwhile simply to note that there are occasional distinctions. In those cases where there are differences, states usually err on the side of being more protective, rather than less, of the rights of the individual shareholders within that state.

Likewise, we will use the New York Stock Exchange as an example of a self-regulatory organization for listed securities. Yes, there are other exchanges—the American Stock Exchange, the Pacific Stock Exchange, the Midwest Stock Exchange, the Philadelphia Stock Exchange, and that government-induced hybrid known as the Cincinnati Exchange, to name just a few— but the NYSE is the best-known of all and, since the companies listed on the NYSE represent collectively a far greater portion of investors' dollars than all other exchanges (something like 80 or 85 percent), we will use it as the representative for all. The National Association of Securities Dealers is the organization we'll look at when discussing unlisted securities, or those which trade over the counter. Finally, we'll take a look at the role of the Federal Reserve Board (The FRB or, in common usage, "the Fed"). While the Fed is not technically a securities rulemaking organization, you can bet your very last paper dollar that your investments are intimately affected by the actions of this organization. Therefore, we'll discuss the role the Fed plays in determining the outcome of the games.

THE SECURITIES AND EXCHANGE COMMISSION

In 1933, primarily as a result of the excesses of individual companies and the investment bankers, brokers, and (at the time) banks which brought them public, Congress enacted the Truth in Securities Act. In 1934 Congress enacted the Securities Exchange Act, which established the Securities and Exchange Commission and charged it with the responsibilty of administering all the provisions of both of these laws. The SEC's initial charter was to make certain that any company offering a new issue fully disclosed all the pertinent facts about itself before allowing it to proceed with the public offering. This applied not only to companies that had never before been traded but also to existing companies that chose to offer new stock or new bonds.

Companies were, from that day forward, required to file a *registration statement* in which they revealed, for the public record, all sorts of information about their financial condition, including their assets and liabilities and their profit and loss records. A registration statement also had to disclose any outstanding securities; to list the company's primary officers and directors, including their salaries and other compensation and any interests they held in terms of an equity position in the stock; and to list all individuals who owned for themselves or beneficially more than 10 percent of any of those securities; and to describe in detail what the company does, what risk considerations are generic to its industry and unique to itself, and its strategy for the future.

Does this mean that you can depend on the information contained in a company's prospectus (a printed form of the registration statement), which the SEC requires be made available to any potential buyer of the new issue? Having considered this question in Chapter 4, we aren't *that* naive. Plainly stated on the first page of every prospectus is the SEC's disclaimer that it passes no judgment whatsoever on whether or not these securities are a good investment or even on whether or not the information contained therein is true or false. The SEC cannot possibly investigate every single new company. It reviews the registration statement to ensure that it contains the minimum disclosure information required, but it doesn't administer polygraph tests.

Since there are criminal penalties for willful failure to disclose germane information or for knowingly disclosing information that is patently false, most companies filing a registration statement will not deliberately misstate any information in the registration statement. Nonetheless, there is still that very, very large gray area wherein a great deal of information is not only subject to interpretation but subject to accounting legerdemain as well. While all prospectuses contain an auditor's opinion as to whether the financial statements contained therein "present fairly the financial position" of the firm being audited and discuss the auditor's opinion as to the "results of their operations," remember that even a Big Eight accounting firm's opinion is just that—an opinion. No matter how well-intentioned, the auditors can report only on what they can uncover. Nonetheless, a favorable opinion from a nationally recognized auditor does—and should—carry more weight than one signed, "Morry, Guido, and the Guys." A prospectus, in short, is merely a source of information; it may or may not be 100 percent accurate or complete. As always, let the buyer beware.

From this early role of attempting to protect the public from shady operators, the SEC has expanded its interests to become, in effect, the policeman the government uses in all aspects of securities industry regulation.

Rather than discuss in detail all the farflung enforcement activities of the SEC, let's just summarize its primary activities. If ever you have a conflict with your brokerage firm in any of the following areas, the SEC has empowered the various exchanges that are registered with it to adjudicate most of these disputes. That's why they are called *self-regulatory organizations*. However, the SEC retains the final decision-making authority over any questionable practice. The SEC's areas of authority include: detecting and halting manipulation of trading prices of securities, fraudulent activities, or manipulative activities like churning or trading without proper authorization; limiting the powers of exchange members when those powers would not be in the best interest of the investing public; supervising adherence to the aforementioned securities registration requirements; establishing reporting documentation (available for public inspection) for publicly traded companies; establishing rules for the use of proxies; and setting the rules for securities firms dealing with the public; determining what minimum net capital and books and records a brokerage firm must have; outlining inside-trading and reporting requirements; and specifying when a securities exchange, a security listed on an exchange, an exchange member, or an exchange officer can be suspended from dealing with the public. These and a host of other, far more obscure powers affect how brokers deal with one another as well as with the public.

While many people believe that the SEC also has rulemaking authority to establish margin requirements, this is in fact the domain of the Federal Reserve Board and of the various exchanges, which we will discuss later in this chapter.

THE SELF-REGULATORY ORGANIZATIONS (SROs)

Given these far-reaching powers, what's left for the NYSE and the other principal exchanges to do as self-regulatory organizations (SROs)? The simplest way of answering this is that, in theory, the SROs make all the rules for their member firms, and the SEC then approves those rules. In fact, the SEC often suggests, sometimes quite strongly, what rules it believes the SROs should make and how they might best be written; the SROs then make and enforce them. That doesn't mean that the SEC can't step in any time it feels that the exchanges aren't doing the proper job, nor does it mean that the exchanges need not inform the SEC of the decisions they have made so that the SEC may review and, in some cases, override them. But it does mean that the exchanges have the responsibility of enforcing a host of rules and regulations that they have placed into effect in order to facilitate customer and broker-to-broker transactions. Have the NYSE, the National Association of Securities Dealers, and the other SROs always fulfilled their policing functions to the SEC's satisfaction? In a word, no. The SEC has made abundantly clear over the years that it felt that the various SROs were just a little too easygoing when it came to disciplining its member firms and their employees. The result has been that, in recent years, the exchanges as well as their member firms have considerably increased their own enforcement capabilities. They were pushed in this direction both by the Amendment Acts of 1964, which the SEC had wanted to see enacted for some time and by the regulations that resulted from the Securities Reform Act of 1975.

Let's face it, the various SROs have a number of constituents to please. On the one hand, they are charged by the SEC with policing their member firms and all the employees of those member firms. On the other hand, they depend on those member firms for continued revenue and existence. Thus, while individual brokers will occasionally be brought to task for churning or high-pressure tactics or abuse of the discretionary authority occasionally vested in them, most of the time member firms are handled with kid gloves. Of course, cases of flagrant abuse or willful fraud are another story. All in all, it's a delicate tightrope that the NYSE and the other SROs must walk in order to remain in existence. Some of their activities in pursuit of these dual goals include: reviewing all forms of communication with the public, including all advertising; providing arbitration services for customers and member firms involved in a dispute (or member firms in disputes with one another); levying fines and other penalties, including suspension, against member firms or their employees who transgress against the rules of the various exchanges; establishing the framework of regulations that permit the orderly transfer of securities; and, on the exchanges, maintaining, through the specialist system, orderly markets in all listed securities.

The National Association of Securities Dealers (NASD) does for the over-the-counter (OTC) markets pretty much what all the various exchanges do for the listed markets. That is, it also may expel or suspend member dealers for fraudulent acts, fictitious transactions, misstatements, failure to produce records, and other transgressions against its rules. Of course, in the OTC markets, there is no specialist system to buy and sell securities. (The NYSE and other exchanges have assigned "specialists"—firms that are taxed with the responsibility of maintaining orderly markets in the trading of a given issue. The best way to think of the way they do this is to consider exchange-listed transactions as an auction. The very best bid to buy and the very best offer to sell are "matched" on the floor. Ten seconds, or two seconds, or twenty seconds later—whenever the next orders come in—the best bid and offer are again matched, and so on.) For OTC stocks, there is a "negotiated" marketplace—which means that various dealers publish the best prices they will pay for a security and the best prices at which they will sell a security, and it's up to the buyer to survey the market and choose the OTC securities dealer with whom he or she will do business on that particular transaction. Of course, you need never be involved in this process; your stockbrokerage firm is supposed to do all this for you. Somewhat greater caution is usually required in dealing with OTC issues than with those listed on an exchange. The requirements for being listed are more stringent than those for being traded OTC. While it's true that a number of fine companies traded OTC could list on an exchange if they chose to, there are also a lot of losers. Be careful.

So what's the net affect of all this on your investing? Which "officials" do you turn to if you feel a rule has been violated? Just as in any sport, while you can complain to any referee, there's always going to be one referee who has the final say. It's the same in securities markets. In this case the final authority is usually the SEC. If you have a problem with a transaction that took place with a member of the NYSE, you will do well to attempt first to resolve your difficulty directly with that firm. The compliance officers of these member firms don't want to get embroiled in a controversy with the SEC or the various exchanges. If, however, you still feel you have been treated shoddily after communicating your concerns directly to the firm, your best bet is to appeal directly to the head ump—in this case, the SEC. I strongly recommend that you also send a copy of your complaint letter to the exchange governing that member firm as well as to the State Securities Commissioner of the state in which you are a resident. It never hurts to have a number of refs reviewing the instant replay (especially the State Securities Commissioner, who will probably view you as a home-team player more than the others will).

What if the problem is with a securities dealership that is not a member of an exchange but is rather a member of the NASD? Same story. Attempt to resolve the problem with the firm first. Failing this, go to the SEC, sending copies of your letter to the State Securities Commissioner and to the NASD.

THE FEDERAL RESERVE BOARD

The last officiating organization we'll discuss is the Federal Reserve Board. It is the Federal Reserve Board that determines what the initial margin requirement will be at any given time as well as for any given security. This means that when the Fed decides that speculation is rampant and must be curbed, it has the right to require that, when buying on margin, you put up a greater percentage of your own money than you would at other times. Right now, this *initial margin requirement* is 50 percent.

This means that, should you decide to purchase 100 shares of a stock selling for $50, you may of course pay for it in full, or $5,000. As you recall from Chapter 2, you may, however, elect to pay only 50 percent of this amount, or $2,500. The brokerage firm will then lend you money, usually at a rate in the neighborhood of ½ to 1½ percent over prime, to allow you to purchase the rest. Should the markets heat up and the Fed decide to put a damper on things, they may decide that the initial margin requirement should be 75 percent—in which case, you could still purchase 100 shares of that $50 stock, but you would have to put up $3,750 and the brokerage firm could you only lend $1,250. While this may be the most obvious role of the Fed, it is by no means the most significant.

The reason we include the Fed in the group of officiating bodies is that the Fed's day-to-day and month-to-month activities so dominate the conduct and outcome of the games in the arena that it is imperative to understand the nature of the beast. The Fed is an absolutely fascinating phenomenon of the twentieth century. Who would have thought, lo those many years ago, when our ancestors threw a few bones into the middle of a circle to predict the future, that we today would devise something as complicated, sophisticated, and all-encompassing as the Federal Reserve Board which would employ hundreds and hundreds of economists? Of course, the fact that the *results* are no better than throwing bones into a circle shouldn't deter us. Remember the old saw, "If you laid all the economists in the world end to end, they still wouldn't reach a conclusion." Just because the Fed's efforts are occasionally impossible to understand or seem ill-conceived, don't you believe for a minute that you should dismiss this organization as the economists' answer to the Keystone Kops. The Fed doesn't have to be right or wrong in order to create havoc. By the same token, it doesn't have to be right or wrong in order to create significant opportunities for those of us who understand, if not its methods, at least the end result of its machinations. By the way, I freely admit that I am not certain that I understand how and why the Fed does what it does in order to determine the amount of money in the economy at any given time. I *am* certain, however, that it doesn't matter, since I *know* that no one else inside or outside the Fed fully understands what it is doing.

The basic distinction between you and me and the Federal Reserve Board is that you and I make *money;* the Fed *makes* money. That is, it literally produces money out of thin air. Nice trick, huh? When you and I try something like that, it's called counterfeiting. When the Fed does it on behalf of the U.S. government, it's called inflation. Let's take a look at just how it does this.

The first concept we need to grasp is that money is like any other commodity: if we have more of it than we need to meet our basic requirements, we use the excess to get something we want—that is, we spend it. If all of us are spending all of our extra money, that means that the goods produced, to some degree, get sold to the highest bidders. If everyone is willing to pay the full retail price for, say, videocassette recorders, and the supply of VCRs is limited, there would be no reason for them to drop in price or to go on sale. As a matter of fact, prices would be likely to go *up,* because those willing to spend the most would get the products. By the same token, if we have very little money, we are going to put off making purchases—in which case, since none of us are buying anything, there's no reason to produce anything, and the country slips into what is politely called a recession. Remember, since only the Fed can make money out of thin air, the rest of us are merely *exchanging* for goods and services the fixed amount of money in the economy at any given time.

What's the net effect of the Fed's actions? Too much money sloshing around the country equals inflation. Too little money in the economy to make purchases and keep the goods and services flowing equals recession. Ideally, the Fed's goal is to have just enough money in the economy to avoid inflation or recession. How successful they've been in doing this we can see by noting that the extent of inflationary and recessionary excesses since 1913, when the Fed was created, is just about the same as it was *before* the Fed was created. (There were 7 such cycles culminating in market crashes from 1813–1913: in 1819, 1837, 1857, 1873, 1883, 1893, and 1907. Depending on who's counting, we're on track to beat that record between 1913 and 2013.) Of course, failure in the federal government has never in itself been reason enough to do away with an established bureaucracy.

There are three basic ways in which the Fed creates money in order to walk the line between recession and inflation. That is, the Fed uses three techniques to increase or decrease the supply of money. In what is probably ascending order of importance, they are the discount rate, the reserve requirement, and open-market operations.

The Discount Rate

For Fed watchers, the fact that the Fed raised its discount rate on September 3, 1987, may have presaged the great Crash of '87. How does the discount rate work? Well, it comes about because the Fed is perceived as "the lender of last resort" to the various commercial banks in the country. This is a relatively recent phenomenon. From 1913 until 1980, only *member banks*—those affiliated with the Federal Reserve System—could borrow at the Federal Reserve's "discount window." But in 1980 the Fed's powers were extended through the Depository Institutions Deregulation and Monetary Control Act. Since then, all banks and all thrift institutions in this country—40,000 or so at last count—have had to go to the Fed if they couldn't get funds from any other source. Even a bank in great condition will occasionally lend out more money than it has assets to lend. When this happens, the bank can turn to the Fed and borrow short term, at the *discount rate*. (Incidentally, the discount rate doesn't refer to a preferential rate but, rather, to the fact that the borrower has reviewed and discounted all other possibilities.) They've chosen the "lender of last resort," discounting all others. When the Fed raises this discount rate, it essentially makes it much more expensive for a bank to borrow. As a result, the bank will probably charge more interest when it lends money and will probably make fewer loans to its customers in order to avoid being in the same position next week. In short order, if the discount rate stays very high, the higher cost of money (passed on to borrowers) and the reduced availability of money act to slow down the pace of business activity. Of course, if the Fed chooses to go in the other direction and reduce the discount rate, banks pick up money at a very competitive rate and can then charge less when they lend to businesses and individuals. Conversely, they can also simply make more loans because they have more money. In either case, this tends to increase the amount of money in the economy, which in turn allows people and businesses to buy things and get the factories and service industries revved up again.

Bankers don't like to go to the Federal Reserve and admit that they've run short of cash. Let's face it, if banks were dumb, they wouldn't have all the money. So, rather than borrow from the Fed, they do a number of things. Multinational banks can bring funds in from branches outside the United States. Banks can sell CDs (and not the $10,000 or $100,000 they would offer to you and me, but millions and millions of dollars in CDs to various corporations). But the best way they have of avoiding going to the Fed is to borrow from other banks that have extra money. To do this, they deal in what is called the *federal funds market,* which consists of nothing more than banks borrowing money from one another. When they do so, they will pay interest at what is called the *federal funds rate*. It sounds in this case as if the Fed is on the outside looking in, doesn't it? Don't bet on it. The Fed not only determines the discount rate but also virtually determines the federal funds rate. It usually does this via its open-market operations, which we'll discuss shortly.

The Reserve Requirement

The second way in which the Fed determines the money supply is by establishing the level of reserves that banks must hold in order to be able to conduct their business. We have created in this country what is called a *fractional reserve system*. It is considered a fractional reserve system not because, no matter how much you make, you're allowed to keep only a fraction of it, but because the banks need to keep only a fraction of the deposits we give them against the day that we'll want our money back. They are free to lend the rest of our money to others and to secure a reasonable rate of return on it. This means that if you give your banker $10,000 to place into your checking account, the banker isn't obliged to keep all $10,000 there just because history and circumstances dictate that by the end of the month you'll have taken the whole $10,000 back out to pay your bills. The reserve requirements vary, but, for a consumer checking account, the Fed will probably make the bank keep available a reserve of only 10 cents or so of every dollar you give it in case you decide to withdraw the entire amount and go to Mexico.

The reserve requirement can be changed at will by the Fed. Now, by definition, if the reserve rate were ever to reach 100 cents on the dollar (which, to the best of my knowledge, it never has), then no bank would be able to make any kind of loan whatsoever. In short order, the banks would have to either charge you significantly higher rates for your checking account or go out of business. But the Fed could move the reserve requirement up or down incrementally; even lowering it to 7 cents on the dollar or raising it to 13 cents on the dollar would make a significant difference in a bank's lendable funds and in its bottom line. What the bank does with all these additional dollars that don't have to be held in reserve is give them to someone else in the form of a loan. Of course, when the bank lends money to someone, the borrowed money is usually simply deposited in another checking or savings account. It may be a checking account at that bank or at someone else's bank, but the money still is just transferred around. Again, remember that money is not being created. There's a fixed amount of it, and all we're doing is transferring it among ourselves.

Open-Market Operations

The third way in which the Fed determines how much money will be in the economy is through its *open-market operations,* which involve the buying and selling of various U.S. government securities. The Fed always deals in U.S. government securities because they are the most abundant securities around and because they are perceived as the most secure. Who at the Fed wants to explain to the boss why they bought General Motors instead of IBM instead of Ford instead of Electronic Gizmo Inc. bonds? They deal mostly in Treasury bills, which mature in less than a year. This is because the Fed is concerned with short-term rates, for the most part. It's also because this is the biggest market of Treasury issues. Something like two-thirds of all Treasury issues traded are Treasury bills.

Okay, here comes the fun part: now we're going to learn how to *make* real money. Let's presume that, for whatever reason, the Fed has decided that there's too little money around. Because of this, bankers aren't making a lot of loans. In order to get money to make what loans they do make, they have to borrow in the federal funds market and are probably paying an arm and a leg to do so. Of course, they are passing along these high costs to their borrowers. Because borrowers have to pay so much to get money, not a lot of them are borrowing. As a result, business activity in general is depressed. (Actually, rightly or wrongly, almost nobody at the Fed thinks we can have another depression; they only talk about recession, so I guess we shouldn't say that the level of business activity is "depressed," let's say it's "recessed.")

What the Fed does, in order to stimulate the economy, is buy Treasury bills, which it has to do the open market. To do this, the Fed calls a few government-bond dealers, lets them know that it's looking, and entertains offers from them to sell Treasury bills back to the Fed. Here's the nifty part: Let's say that the Fed has decided it wants to buy $500 million worth of Treasury bills. The traders at the Fed simply tell the government-bond dealer that they are buying and, upon consummation of the deal, they may add $500 million to the bond dealer's bank account. Where do the Fed's traders get the $500 million? They make it. That is, they create it out of nothing. It isn't secured by gold, mansions, potatoes, corn flakes, or any other commodity. But let's take a look at what happens when that $500 million gets credited to the government-bond dealer's bank account. The bond dealer no longer has the bonds, but it does have $500 million cash on deposit. In effect, the bank that has the dealer's checking account has an extra $500 million. They must keep some percentage of this against the eventuality of withdrawals, but the rest of it they can use to make loans to businesses, to individuals, or to other banks. Since the bank now has $500 million sloshing about and wants to get some return on it, it's likely to be a tad more aggressive than other banks would be and take a bit less in interest in order to get that money working for it. You can see that if the Fed does this with 10 government-bond dealers for $500 million each, we're talking about some serious new money. By creating new money in the form of reserves in a bank's various accounts, the Fed can depress the federal funds rate and, by making money cheaper, get people to borrow more easily and spend more freely.

Of course, conversely, if the Fed decides that we're having entirely too much fun with all this money or that inflation is getting out of hand, it simply removes reserves from the various banks. It does this by *selling* $500 million worth of Treasury bills to the government-bond dealer. When it does this, it deducts the $500 million from that dealer's checking account at the bank. The dealer now has $500 million in Treasury bills, but the government, in the form of the Fed, has removed $500 million from the banking system. Of course, that $500 million was the basis for quite a few more loans that the bank had made. Now the bank has to hold off making new loans, which in turn depresses business activity. It may even call in or not roll over some outstanding loans. If this bank now has to go into the federal funds market, it may be faced with having to pay so much for federal funds that it is more attractive to call in a few loans. It's certainly going to be more attractive to refrain from making new loans. You can see that these open-market operations permit the Fed to manipulate the federal funds rate pretty much at its whim.

Okay, so the Fed can create an inflationary or recessionary environment. How does this affect us as investors? In two ways. First, we are no longer willing to buy on margin (borrowing money from our brokers) because interest rates in an inflationary environment are so high that it skews our risk-reward ratios. Also, there's not much reason to risk our money in the stock market at all if we can get a 15 percent return on a government-guaranteed Treasury bill. The second and more important consideration is that the stock market reacts strongly to inflationary or recessionary expectations. If the Fed has created lots of money, then there's lots of money to chase stocks. If there isn't much money in the system, there isn't money to chase stocks and the market will go down.

The lesson to learn from all this is: if you are going to play the game successfully, you must pay attention to what the Fed does. If you see articles and statistics telling you that the Federal Reserve Board has raised the discount rate, raised the reserve requirement, or is selling significant quantities of Treasury bills, notes, and bonds in the open market, look out! The Fed is signaling that it's going to be taking money out of the nation's economy. If the market has been roaring ahead, this reduction in money available to chase stocks will put a damper on the party. If, however, at the bottom of one of the next few recessions, you read that the Fed has dropped the discount rate, lowered the reserve requirement, or is purchasing Treasury bills, notes, and bonds, it's probably time to get into the stock market. Since the daily headlines will still be dreadful, you've got time to jump on board before the train picks up steam. Don't be swayed by the number of pronouncements you read from "the experts" telling you that this time is different, that we're in a "new era" and therefore the actions of the Fed don't mean anything. Bull. When I see the Fed attempting to pump lots of money into the nation's banking system, that's an early indicator that other people are going to have a lot of money to expand their businesses and chase stocks. Conversely, when I see that the Fed is doing everything it can to pull funds away from consumers and businesses, it's time for me to get out of the market, no matter how exciting the front-page headlines may be. I am not interested in someone's pronouncements that we are in a new era, I'm interested in what is really happening. It isn't what they say that counts, it's what they do.

That about does it for the various referees, umpires, and watchdogs. These are the organizations and agencies that not only make the rules but also enforce them. Their decisions affect how we play the game and therefore, whether we win or lose. While the regulatory bodies determine the actual official rules, there are more important rules than the official rules in sports, in life, and in investing—so let's move on to our final precompetition area: the ethics of the game.

CHAPTER 7

ETHICS: HOW YOU PLAY
THE GAME

All right, competitors, this is important: there's a right way and a wrong way to play these games. The right way is to shoot straight with other people, treat 'em right and expect the same in return. The wrong way is any other way. Now, as we said in Chapter 5, unless you buy only no-load mutual funds and then only directly from the mutual fund company itself, you're going to have to have an account with a brokerage firm. Even if you deal only with a mutual fund or only with an investment counselor, there are still some important things to remember along the way.

The most important of these is that the stock market is one of the last remaining "verbal contract" businesses left in America. Therefore, it is important for the success of the game that all parties be of the highest ethical caliber and that they honor any commitment made to each other. Okay, so the chances of this happening in every single transaction are roughly the same as the probability that the Love Boat will cruise to Vladivostok this winter for fun in the sun. It should, nonetheless, happen most times out. Why? Because it's in the best interests of brokerage firms or advisors to be straightforward in their dealings with their customers. There are those who would disagree with me. Richard Ney, in the preface to his thought-provoking book, *The Wall Street Jungle,* retells the story that gangster Lucky Luciano, after being deported to Italy, granted an interview in which he told about a visit he had made to the New York Stock Exchange. After the intricacies of the responsibilities and rewards of the NYSE specialists had been explained, he supposedly said that, right then and there, "I realized I'd joined the wrong mob." Of course, there are some things you can do to ensure that your relationship with your broker or other financial advisors/coaches is as honest and aboveboard as possible.

When you open a brokerage account, you must usually sign a written agreement stating, among other things, that you will accept responsibility for any order you place with your brokerage firm. Now, if a question arises about whether you did or did not place an order or about the time or price at which you placed it, you as well as the brokerage firm must be as good as your word. When you place an order to buy, you tacitly give your word that you will pay for the stock. When you place an order to sell, you implicitly promise that, if you hold the stock certificates, you will deliver them promptly.

Why is this verbal contract so important? Buying and selling securities is not like buying a piece of merchandise at a retail store and later changing your mind, in which case the store owner can send the merchandise back to the manufacturer for a full refund or a credit or future purchases. When your stockbrokerage firm acts on your instructions and buys stock for your account, the stock is not usually coming from a shelf in the back room but from another person like yourself or, if your transaction is a sizeable one, perhaps from a small institution. (The only exception to this is those stocks which trade over the counter. In these cases, the brokerage firm may or may not already have an "inventory" of shares in the issue you are interested in. This is done for two reasons. First, in the case of a "thinly traded" security, it makes it easier for you to acquire the security. It would be more time-consuming and probably more costly to you if the brokerage firm had to seek out an individual who had these shares to sell. Second, of course, the brokerage firm, by carrying these shares in inventory, stands to make a small profit between the price it paid to acquire them and the price at which it sells them to you.) It is important to understand that in all cases, whether the brokerage firm buys the stock for your account on one of the exchanges or buys it from another broker or carries it in inventory, it must *purchase* the stock, spending its own capital. They take responsibility for paying for it.

TRADE CONFIRMATIONS

Once you agree to buy securities, you are normally given five business days to pay for your purchase. A *trade confirmation* is ordinarily, as a matter of courtesy, sent to the investor. This trade confirmation gives you the full particulars of your transaction, including the date of purchase and the settlement date, the name of the security, the number of shares purchased (or sold), the price at which they were purchased (or sold), the amount of the commission charged, the total amount due to the brokerage firm (or, in the case of a sale, the amount due to you) and the market where the order was executed.

Remember, a trade confirmation is not a bill! In this verbal contract business, just as you may give your order in person or by phone rather than in writing, the brokerage firm need not ensure that you receive *written* notification of the transaction; your monthly statement does that, but only at month-end. On the day of your transaction, representatives of the brokerage firm attempt to reach you. If you are unavailable and are not made aware of the transaction, this does *not* relieve you of the responsibility to honor your purchase or sale. Most brokerage firms endeavor to notify their clients both verbally and in writing. However, if you are unavailable, you must remember that you have only five business days from the date of the transaction, not from the date the brokerage firm finally finds you at home. Being out of town (or successfully evading your broker!) doesn't absolve you of responsibility. Remember, therefore, if you plan to be on vacation or to change your address or will be unavailable for any other reason, it is your responsibility to inform the brokerage firm or firms to which you have given orders.

Some brokerage firms will occasionally extend the settlement date by two days. This is done as a courtesy and should not be expected on anything akin to a regular basis. Beyond these two extra days, the brokerage firm must petition the various exchanges for the right to extend the settlement date further. These *extensions* are not automatically granted; an extension request must be made for a very good reason. Why are the exchanges so tough about allowing extensions? Partly because the brokerage firms, who pay annual dues to keep the exchanges running, want them to be, but also because, by not paying on time, you violate the Federal Reserve Board's Regulation T, which covers the extension of credit on securities transactions.

These regulations are designed to prevent, among other things, free-riding.

Free-riding is the term used when a firm or an individual enters an order to buy a stock but then honors the commitment only if the price of the stock rises. If the price of the stock falls, this unethical investor disavows the transaction. A variation on this trick, and the one that gave rise to the term, is the situation in which an investor places a buy order with broker A and then, if the stock rises before settlement date, sells the stock through broker B. The investor then requests an early payout (some brokerage firms will occasionally grant such payouts for bona-fide emergencies) and uses the proceeds of the sale to pay for the buy. As a result, of course, the investor has gotten a "free ride" by entering into a riskless—albeit illegal and unethical— transaction. In another variation, an investor buys stock XYZ from broker A on Tuesday and sells the same stock through the same broker on Thursday without ever having intended to pay for the transaction. *Any* such activity is illegal and is considered a fraudulent transaction. In all the above cases, remember—if you can't do the time, don't do the crime. If you are late in paying, you are, in the eyes of the Fed, potentially guilty of free-riding. This is a violation of federal law and will land you in jail as surely as tax fraud or a backyard whiskey still. Don't risk it! Enter into all transactions in good faith, expect the brokerage firm to do the same, pay for your transactions on time, and expect your broker to do the same.

DELIVERY OF CERTIFICATES

It is equally incumbent upon your broker to act in good faith in all other areas. That is, the firm must properly execute all orders as soon as possible after you have given the order, report the results to you if at all possible, and, if you are selling, credit your account or provide you with a check on settlement date, five business days after the sale. If you are purchasing, and for some reason wish to take possession of the actual certificates, the brokerage firm must instruct the transfer agent as soon as funds are received from you that it is okay to transfer the security and mail it to you. The length of time it will take for you to receive your certificate varies, depending on a number of factors: how high the level of general market activity is, how many issues the transfer agent is responsible for, how skilled the transfer agent is, whether you paid on time, and whether your broker entered instructions in a timely manner. Ordinarily, you can expect to receive your certificates from three to five weeks after the brokerage firm receives your funds.

By the way, few investors and virtually no investment professionals take physical delivery of their stock certificates. I don't, for one. I don't need to see the piece of paper issued by the company to have proof that I own the stock, any more than I need to keep all my cash under my mattress to have proof that it's there. I find it more convenient to write a check for my mortgage every month than to pay in cash, so I keep my cash in the bank. The deposit receipt and monthly statement are all I need. By the same token, I find it far more convenient to keep my securities with my broker; I have trade confirmations and monthly statements that, like the bank's statements, constitute evidence of my ownership. This way, I don't have to rent a safe deposit box, deliver certificates, and so on. The big difference is that my dollars in the bank are insured only up to $100,000. The stocks I keep at my brokerage firm are protected by the Securities Investors Protection Corporation, an agency of the federal government, up to $500,000, of which $100,000 may be in cash and still be covered. Additional protection may also be available from your brokerage firm.

OPENING THE RIGHT TYPE OF ACCOUNT

Your brokerage firm takes on faith that you understand the level of trading or investing you have chosen to engage in and that you are in fact one of the individuals named in the agreement allowed to do business in your account. The most common forms of agreements between investors and brokerage firms are:

1. *Individual account.* You and only you have any interest in or authority over the transactions that occur in the account.

2. *Joint tenants "with right of survivorship."* This type of account is usually entered into by a married couple. Should one party die, all assets in the account are presumed to be left to the surviving party (hence the term "rights of survivorship").

3. *Tenants in common.* If one party dies, his or her share of the assets of the account are presumed to be a part of his or her estate and are transferred ultimately to his or her heirs, *not* to the surviving party who also signed the agreement.

4. *Custodian account.* In recent years many investors have chosen to make gifts of securities to their minor children. While the law allows many different types of securities to be placed into custodian accounts, such an account is established for the benefit of the child, so the investments purchased in this type of account should be those deemed most prudent for anticipated growth and safety. Any leveraging is proscribed in this type of account; that is, you, the custodian, can't lose more than you put up and indebt the child by buying on margin so that when the child reaches the age of majority, he or she actually *owes* money. Accordingly, only cash transactions may be entered into in a custodian account.

5. *Investment club account.* A number of individuals band together and contribute (usually) small amounts of money, pooling their resources so that they can purchase more shares or issues than each member could afford on his or her own. Each of these investment clubs designates a limited number of its members to act as agents for the club in buying and selling securities with the brokerage firm—sort of like a mutual fund without the regulations and (usually) without full-time management. Many of these clubs have done exceedingly well over the years. The National Association of Investment Clubs (NAIC) can help you get started if you're interested in joining or organizing an investment club. The NAIC is dedicated to the proposition that small doesn't mean powerless!

6. *Partnership account.* This type of account is opened by a

much smaller number of investors (usually two), each of whom has equal authority to act as agent for the account.

7. *Trust account.* Assets are held in the name of a trust, which may be formed to benefit one individual or a group of individuals or a particular cause. Brokerage firms regularly accept trust accounts, but the agreements establishing the trust are best handled by an attorney. If you have established a trust, you already know that. If you haven't, and are considering it, you're going to need the help of a competent attorney. There is no sense in delving into the intricacies of trust accounts here. We have a deal with the legal profession—we don't practice law and they don't write investment books. (At least we *keep* our part of the bargain!)

8. *Corporation account.* Corporations opening such accounts may be either for-profit or nonprofit corporations, and legal evidence of incorporation must accompany not only the initial application but also the transfer of shares. Your broker will help you with the necessary paperwork.

The brokerage firm should also assist you when you are deciding whether to open a cash, cash and margin, or cash, margin, and option account. In a *cash account,* you agree to pay in full for all brokerage firm transactions within the prescribed five business days. To review, if you open a *margin account,* the brokerage firm extends you a certain amount of credit. For example, you purchase XYZ stock. You put up one-half the total purchase price, and the brokerage firm lends you the other half. Remember, the amount the brokerage firm lends you is determined not by the individual brokerage firm, but by the Fed. Currently, if you purchase $6,000 worth of securities in a margin account, the Fed allows the brokerage firm to lend you as much as $3,000 (50 percent) of this amount. The brokerage firm uses the stock you have just purchased as collateral for the $3,000 loan. The amount the brokerage firm may lend can be changed by the Fed at any time. There are no individual variations among brokerage firms; the Fed's loan regulations apply to all firms. Remember, the leverage you gain by purchasing on margin cuts both ways: in a rising market, you benefit from the increase on a smaller dollar amount actually out of pocket; in a declining market, you lose capital at a rate far greater, given the amount of capital invested. This is merely a loan from your broker, not an equity participation. Your brokerage firm just deals in this casino, it doesn't play.

If you choose to deal in *stock options* or *index options,* the brokerage firm will ask you a number of personal questions that they would not have to ask merely to establish a cash or margin account. The reason for this is that trading in options is potentially a highly speculative activity. While it is true that writing covered options does not fit into this "speculative" category, when buying options or entering into spreads or straddles or combination-type orders, you *can* lose as much as 100 percent of your investment. When writing uncovered options or short straddles, you *can* lose many hundreds, thousands, or tens of thousands of percent more than your original investment. This point is brought home more clearly when we talk in dollar terms rather than percentage terms. How'd you like to scrape together $10,000 and, virtually in one day, owe $1 million? Welcome to the wonderful world of naked options. Accordingly, the more risky the transaction in options, the more stringent the suitability and knowledgeability requirements that brokerage firms levy upon their clients. While the brokerage firm has an ethical responsibility not to allow you to engage in transactions for which you are ill-suited or lack the financial wherewithal, it is ultimately your responsibility to portray your financial condition and knowledge of these securities honestly and accurately to the brokerage firm.

Simply by opening their doors and thereby agreeing to Securities and Exchange Commission supervision, brokerage firms are aware that it's in their best interest to deal honestly and ethically with the investment public. In addition to SEC supervision, brokerage firms are regulated by some or all of the following: the Federal Reserve Board, state securities commissioners, the New York Stock Exchange, the National Association of Securities Dealers, other regional exchanges, or other self-regulatory organizations. Compliance with federal regulations as well as rules of business conduct and fair practice are outlined for them. Do brokerage firms always comply with these regulations and rules of ethical conduct? No. Just as there are unethical investors, there are unethical brokers. The vast majority of brokers realize that there is no need for dishonesty. It's an amazingly profitable business when done straight, so why bother to do it crooked? This is Big Casino and they are, after all, The House.

Does this mean brokers are always on the investor's side? No. But for the most part they operate according to "enlightened self-interest." It is safe to assume that your brokerage firm does not wish to run afoul of federal regulations or to get the bad press that results from poor investor relations. Remember, however, that when it comes to recommendations made by an *individual* broker on commission, the self-interest may not be so enlightened. Brokers are salespersons; if the broker earns X more dollars by selling product A than product B, he or she will probably sell A.

All the comments in this chapter regarding your relationship with your stockbroker apply equally appropriately to any investment counseling firm, money manager, mutual fund, or other financial firm you deal with. Treat them right, expect the same in return, and don't be shy about letting them know if you feel they have violated their part of the agreement.

Now that we've got a solid grounding in the basics, it's time to step into the starting blocks. As a first step, even before the starting gun is fired, let's steal a glance at the competitors in the blocks next to us.

PART 2

INTO THE BLOCKS: LET THE GAMES BEGIN!

CHAPTER 8

WHO ARE OUR COMPETITORS?

Assessing the Other Players

If we divide our competitors into the various types of institutions and individual investors according to the approach they take to investing, the basic truths don't change. Some competitors are "fundamentalists" who look primarily at a company's earnings, book value, management, and the various disclosure documents (annual reports, quarterly statements, and the like) in order to separate what they believe will be the winning from the losing companies. Other competitors are "technicians" (with and without techniques), who believe that all those factors a fundamentalist looks at, as well as numerous other data regarding the way in which the market views that company and its industry, are already factored into the price of the stock, and instead look primarily at various types of charts and other graphically presented trends for shares of a company's stock. Remember, what it all comes down to is this: there are those who run with the pack and those who run ahead of it.

Just as in the decathlon, those who run with the pack and those who run ahead of it can be of any nationality or background, may use different techniques to win, and may have coaches with distinctly different backgrounds and philosophies. Make no mistake: there are a number of paths to investment success, but the basics don't change. What matters most in the final analysis is the type of coaching you've received, how well you have dedicated yourself to your training, how well you understand the competition, and whether you are in fact willing to distance yourself from the pack. With that in mind, let's take a look at our competitors.

A FEW WORDS ABOUT INSTITUTIONAL INVESTORS

In previous chapters we discussed a number of institutional investors, like mutual funds and investment counseling firms. Other types of institutional investors are: corporate pension funds; bank trust departments; banks dealing for their own accounts; various foundations established by wealthy individuals and corporations; college and university endowment funds; insurance companies; state, federal, and municipal pension plans; and foreign investors represented by large banks and brokers. We've also pointed out that institutional money managers *as a group* do no better than individual investors. That's not to say that there are not a number of institutional money managers who consistently, year in and year out, do better than the market averages. We've spoken about some of these people already, and we'll discuss them and others more fully when we select our winning strategies. Remember, however, as in all endeavors in life, there are very few who run well in front of the pack. Most are content merely to run *with* the pack. This is as true for institutional investors as for individual investors. So what edge do the institutional investors enjoy? There are three supposed advantages.

First, because they are large investors, institutions are better "covered" than individual shareholders are by brokerage firm research departments. Brokers regularly inundate institutional investors with the latest information. It's up to you to decide whether you truly believe this is a benefit or not. I do not. I believe that what often results is mere clutter, chatter and noise that can prevent the recipient from seeing the simple, straightforward facts of a situation.

The second supposed edge institutional investors have is that they have the latest electronic gadgets, which allow them to keep up with global markets from second to second. Again, the same skepticism applies. I'm completely unconvinced that reacting to second-to-second blips in the marketplace is worthwhile. In many cases, the most successful investors of all, institutional or individual, reside in communities far removed from the financial nerve centers of the world and, in fact, often refuse even to look at the market more than once a day. They realize that the market goes through numerous gyrations during each day, some of which may end up being meaningful, but most of which are merely the tug and pull of market activity. Well-placed stop orders can give at least some protection against even a 508-point single-day shift.

The final advantage that institutions supposedly have is their greater access to hot new issues. In this, they do have an edge. If an issue is truly "hot," brokers will always give the lion's share of it to their larger customers in hopes of getting more commissions from these large customers in the future. In the last few years, Apple Computer, Genentech, and Home Shopping Network are examples of companies that were heralded before their initial public offering, sought after by many investors, and parceled out to only a few. If you think that your broker is going to offer you, an individual investor, significant shares of a hot new issue, you might want to consider sharing some of what you've been smoking with the rest of us. The basic rule is that if an issue is really hot, you can't get it; conversely, if you can get it, it's likely to be a lukewarm performer at best. But even though the large institutions do receive preferential treatment in the hot new issues, this advantage really doesn't make much difference. This is hardly the foundation on which you want to build your future investing career. Besides, in many cases, the institutions are so completely diversified that receiving these hot issues doesn't significantly help their overall performance. Even with the occasional minuscule advantage of hot issues, most institutions do no better and no worse than the individual.

It's important to remember, too, that most institutions do well in bull markets and poorly in bear markets. Only the very best hold their own in down markets. Why is this? Well, we have to remember that most institutions remain fully invested through good markets and bad. Most institutions charge management fees based on the amount of assets under management. While you as an individual can (and generally should withdraw from the marketplace or sell short during bear markets, the large institutional money managers don't have this kind of flexibility. Many of them have convinced themselves that, since it's so difficult to time the market, why bother? They've convinced themselves that a buy and hold strategy is the only way to make money in the market over the long term. And, for them, that may be true. But, as an individual, you can strike more quickly and move in and out more easily. Of course, there is also a potential conflict of interest here for institutional money managers: if a fund decided to withdraw from the market completely, then there would be no need for management of the funds, since they would probably be sitting in Treasury bills and other short-term instruments. If that's all the institutional managers are going to do, most investors would withdraw their invested dollars because they'd figure, rightly or wrongly, that they could do as well or better on their own. And if the institutions lose investment dollars and don't keep assets under management, they receive no management fee income.

There is yet another reason that institutional investors should be regarded as "just another competitor." You and I, when confronted with a security that has not fulfilled any of our investment expectations, can quickly sell our stock in a company that just isn't working out. In a major decline, we can also sell short, should we choose to. In many cases, we *would* choose to. Yet not only do institutions not have this opportunity to sell short (it's usually restricted by their charter, bylaws, and covenants) but, since they have a larger position, it's often difficult for them to sell quickly. *Most institutions are battleships, with lots of firepower but limited maneuverability.* Individual investors can hit and run before the battleship can turn.

One other edge that many people believe institutions have is "the best and the brightest" on their staffs. And this may be so. A number of highly educated professionals work for the major institutional money managers. Remember, however, that an advanced degree in economics or business is no protection against "the madness of crowds." Hotshot money managers, with or without advance degrees, are still human. If they are psychologically or emotionally incapable of taking action, it doesn't matter a tinker's dam whether they are intellectually convinced that they should take a certain action. They have to feel it in their gut and have the conviction to stand alone when necessary often when all their peers disagree with them. The secret is not merely being able to analyze and know *what* to do, but being able to *do* it.

Of course, some individual investors shouldn't be playing the market for themselves but *should* have their money professional managed. Because of their financial circumstances (they may have very little to invest and not be able to achieve sufficient diversification for safety) or because they have no time to devote to it or because they may be psychologically unsuited to playing the market, they should let someone else do it for them. Self-knowledge is crucial. If you know that you're just not psychologically suited to break away from the pack, then you will want to find an institutional manager who *is*.

In short, know the institutional investors but, for heaven's sake, don't fear them. You can move in and out faster and, by not being exposed to daily doses of radioactive rumor, can think more clearly. There are some truly gifted individuals in the ranks of money managers, but institutional investors generally *represent* the pack and can only hold you back. They run pretty much together and are uncomfortable about straying too far from the consensus of their peers. You don't want consensus— you want to break away. When it's time to make your move, you need to run ahead of the pack, not with it.

PROGRAM TRADERS

Some institutions and substantial individuals should be feared—not for their prowess, but for their ability to muck up the playing field for the rest of us. While most of its practitioners deny it, those engaging in index arbitrage, portfolio insurance, and other techniques of "hedging" their investments can disrupt the progress of the game in pursuit of a few short-term dollars, increasing the volatility to such an extent that only other "players" with high-speed computers and billions of dollars can survive. Program trading, particularly strategies that use megacomputers and megabucks to play both sides of the market, using common stocks on one side and index futures on the other, is a relatively recent phenomenon.

As a result of this type of activity, many individual investors feel as if they're playing in a rigged game. I'm certain that, faced with an exodus from the stock markets on the part of individual investors (whose pension, savings, and insurance combine to form these institutional juggernauts), Congress, the regulators, or the self-regulatory organizations will have to move to control these legal—but destructive—activities. As a matter of fact, some efforts to restrict volatility have already been implemented. The best-known of these are probably the recently enacted trading halts, which are coordinated between the various stock and futures exchanges and the NYSE's decision to restrict the use of its designated order turnaround (SU-PERDOT) system on days that the Dow Jones Industrial Average moves 25 points or more. Smaller individual orders now have priority use of the NYSE's computerized order system. Program traders must get in line behind them. When the computer at the NYSE can't come out and play, the computers at the program-trading institutions have no one to play with. A few of the institutions have enough brokers on the floors of the various exchanges that they could enter all those orders the old-fashioned way—by using human beings. But, even then, it's not a great feeling to have been selling futures electronically and now be scurrying about trying to buy stocks to secure the sold position bit by bit. That's called exposure, and exposure is a wet blanket on the game of scalping and skimming.

READERS AND CHARTERS

Regardless of whether your competitors are individuals or institutions, most will follow one of two primary methods in analyzing their investments. They will consider themselves either technicians or fundamentalists. Technicians claim that they in fact base their decisions on investor psychology because the sentiments of the crowd are reflected in the technical indicators. Well, maybe so and maybe not. In any race, we don't care about the current pace—we care about timing our bursts so as to pull away from the pack and all our competitors. Technicians, for the most part, monitor the velocity and direction of the pack. They are following the trend; only the best of them break away from the trend.

Fundamentalists, of course, also say that they are students

of market psychology because, in addition to studying the fundamentals of individual companies, they study the fundamentals of the economy, such as the actions of the Federal Reserve Board, the White House, foreign investors, and so on. This may be true, but most fundamentalists put so much emphasis on the individual company that they are often unaware of the fundamental trends emerging in the economy itself.

Fundamentalists

If they are worth their salt, fundamentalists look at corporate management and finances, fiscal and monetary policies, international events, inflation and interest rates, and government actions that can influence the marketplace. Remember, half to five-eighths of all success in the market is determined by the trend of the overall market, and a quarter to three-eighths of it depends on the success of the industry. That leaves a relatively paltry fraction for each individual company to affect its stock's price. That's not to say we shouldn't look at corporate fundamentals, especially in depressed markets. When the market has steadily been going down and the industry group has gone down with it, in order to find the best companies in which to invest for the next turn upward, we want to find those companies which are essentially well-managed and well-capitalized. Mostly, however, it's the economic fundamentals that we should be most interested in. Even then, how the stock market should react to information and how it does react are often two very different things.

Earnings per share, which is the most often quoted and followed fundamental indicator of a company's success or failure, is the foundation on which most fundamentalists base their opinions about which securities to buy and which to sell. This is problematical. Projected earnings often have little relevance to tomorrow's stock price. We have to be careful because we are dealing in the past, present, and future here, and it's easy to confuse the three. The *current* earnings really reflect the past 12 months' earnings. Why in heaven's name I would want to believe that tomorrow's stock price depends on yesterday's earnings reported today is beyond me. Yet people do it all the time. As a matter of fact, the emphasis of most institutional money managers, as well as of the research departments of most brokerage firms, has always been on factors like this. Otherwise intelligent people who would not bet on the outcome of the next role of the dice or the next card to turn up at a blackjack table will invest their life's savings on the basis of some "expert's" view of what earnings will be for some company next year. A price-earnings ratio, which we'll discuss in a later chapter, can be of some value—but fluctuations up a dime or down a quarter in declared earnings per share? Not valuable. Corporate earnings are just too slippery to use in forecasting the future when corporate management can substantially change "earnings" simply by changing the method of accounting for depreciation from straight-line to accelerated or by interpreting the term "depreciation" differently or by funneling money from one subsidiary to another.

Bearing in mind the relationship between economic fundamentals and politics, however, is a whole other thing. I pay a *great deal* of attention to the fundamentals here. When it comes to politics, Americans want a larger-than-life figure as their president. We believe that a strong, fearless leader at the top will help us get through anything. As a result, it behooves us all to pay attention to whether investors truly believe that their elected officials, especially the president, are the kind of leaders who can see us through the tough times. This is a fundamental piece of economic analysis that must be done by all of us. The same economic numbers under a president who is perceived as ineffective will have a radically different effect on stock prices than under a president perceived as effective.

As we've previously discussed in talking about the role of the Fed, the nation's money supply is also terribly important for us to analyze. When lots of money is sloshing around the system, people have extra money and feel rich and are willing to invest in the stock market. When the Fed makes the decision to cut back on the money supply, people feel poor and in fact have less money. This simple information may be our single most important indicator of how well the market should perform in the coming months.

Technicians

If you thought individual corporate fundamentals—annual reports, quarterly reports, and pronouncements from management—were slippery, wait until you see the worlds of wonder created by technical stock analysts. Basically, technicians are on the right track. They attempt to gauge the emotional state of the marketplace at any given point. This is a valuable and valid pursuit; it's also one that, as we have said, is essential to success in the marketplace. The problem is that some technicians forget the forest in their pursuit of individual trees. Technical analysis is nothing more than the study of the actions of stocks themselves instead of the study of the values on which the stocks are supposed to rest. Technicians like to claim that their charts, since they are graphic representations of what's really happening in the marketplace, actually encompass fundamental concepts—that is, that the market has already taken into account every bit of fundamental information and therefore technicians get the best of both worlds.

There is much that I like about technical analysis. Charting the actions of the Fed, member shorts, insider trading, odd lotters, and the like is a very valuable exercise. I don't do it myself, because I find it entirely too time-consuming. A number of investment advisors who write investment newsletters do a superb job of technical analysis. I've already mentioned Bob Gross of *The Professional Investor* and Stan Weinstein of *Professional Tape Reader*. I'll add Martin Zweig of *The Zweig Forecast* as yet another brilliant market technician. Do I suffer by not running my own numbers? Nope—especially since virtually all investment newsletters these days have telephone hot lines that I can call at any time and get a good idea of what the technical indicators say the market is doing. Again, I don't want to overreact. I like to make decisions based on the events of a few days or weeks, not the most recent few hours.

I don't personally select individual companies in which to invest on the basis of that company's chart. As a matter of fact, many of the supposed patterns that some technicians see in their various charts remind me of nothing so much as throwing bones in a circle. The significance of the various triangles, head-and-shoulder patterns, wedges, flags, pennants, islands, scallops, saucers, diamonds, *V*s, *W*s, and *VW*s, saucer tops, saucer bottoms, squiggles, doodles, and what's-its is all too often "in the eye of the beholder." I see no problem with charting the action of the Dow Jones Industrials or a number of other commonly utilized indicators, but I'm darned if I'm going to take the time to construct point and figure charts, bar charts, and trend-line analysis on individual issues. I'm also highly skeptical of support and resistance levels. A support level is the price that a stock supposedly goes down to but seldom penetrates. If it does, this is called a "downside breakout" or a "breakdown." By the same token, a stock is supposed to seldom penetrate its upper "resistance zone." If it does so, this is called an "upside breakout." (It's also called an "uh-oh" if you actually have a position on either side.) In fact, stocks so regularly penetrate their supposed resistance and support levels that the value of these indicators is questionable. I'm also wary of seeing "patterns" where none exist. One that has gotten a great deal of press recently is the "January Indicator." In 38 of the past 58 years, a rising market in January "predicted" an up year for the market. Pretty neat indicator, huh? Well, not so fast. The market rises about two-thirds of the time, so if you'd just guessed that the market would rise *every* year, you'd have been correct *39* out of 58 times.

There are, however, a number of broader-based technical indicators that we may wish to pay attention to. The Dow Jones Industrial Average is, itself, merely a chart of the action of 30 blue-chip industrial stocks. Putting something like this in graphic representation on a chart is very helpful. Not only that, I'm more than happy to let a Bob Gross or a Stan Weinstein do my homework for me. Time is money—I'm happy to give them a little of the latter to save a lot of the former.

A number of theories come along regularly that purport to allow us to interpret market activity on the basis of technical analysis. The best-known of these, and one that I believe has earned a great deal of credibility, is Dow theory. Basically, this theory is very straightforward. It simply states that major bull markets are kicked off when both the Dow Jones Industrial Average and the Dow Jones Transportation Average "break out" (there's that term again) to new high ground. Conversely, major bear markets begin when both the Dow Jones Industrial Average and the Dow Jones Transportation Average go below their previous low points. Dow theory may not always give us the holy grail we seek, but it's been quite helpful in a number of markets over the past half-century or so.

All kinds of other fads come and go. They sell newsletters and may or may not have any real value. Some gurus of the marketplace are very good for a period of time. Unfortunately, however, most of them fall by the wayside after one complete market cycle. When I was just starting out in this business, I studied "on-balance volume," "advance-decline divergences," and all kinds of other arcane information because at that time Joe Granville and Edson Gould were the two reigning gurus. But when Joe Granville started predicting the next earthquake on the basis of his charts, I began to realize that my time might have been better spent.

I don't discount the value of technical analysis. I believe that I need to hire, by subscribing to certain newsletters, analysts who can save me some time by helping me select individual issues and who keep track of the broad trends affecting the economy and the stock market. I just take what they all say with a grain of salt.

Regardless of whether investors are institutional or individual and regardless of whether they think they are using technical or fundamental or psychological measurements, most still run with the pack. Greed and fear are still the two greatest motivators of all our competitors in the investment arena. That's probably why people buy in haste and repent at leisure. In their other business endeavors they may be able to move decisively; in investing, greed pushes them in and fear keeps them from taking action when it's time to sell. One of the most effective ways to distance ourselves from the pack is to recognize when it's no longer intelligent to hold on to a stock or an entire portfolio of stocks and then to be able to make up our minds to sell them. I believe some competitors actually have some kind of psychological desire to lose money. I have seen, time and again, people who consider themselves in their hearts to be losers, also lose in the investment arena. (Maybe Freud was right—people lose in order to punish themselves!)

At any rate, members of the pack always feel most comfortable, regardless of motivation, when running alongside other members of the pack. We may not be able to predict individual response to a certain stimulus, but we can be pretty sure that, *as a group,* they'll react a certain way. Many of them, looking for the next Xerox, will never succeed because they are willing to play only the 100-to-1 shots. Others buy the latest rumor or story. Still others buy so many stocks that they might as well be running an individual mutual fund when in fact they can't keep up with any one issue.

RANDOM WALK THEORISTS

There is a final group of competitors that we need to be aware of. These people have elevated the art of running with the pack to an art form. I'm referring to those academics who espouse the "random walk" theory. You may not think much of the theory, but you've just got to appreciate the pun. Used by Yale professor Burton Malkiel in his book, *A Random Walk Down Wall Street,* the theory basically proposes that stock prices tomorrow are in no way influenced by stock prices today or yesterday—that there is always a 50–50 chance, at the opening bell of the exchange on any given day, that a stock price will either continue to follow the trend it's in or reverse that trend. The underlying idea is that whenever you flip a coin, there's a 50–50 chance that it will come up heads, no matter what's happened before. Random walk theorists believe that, fundamentally, technically, or psychologically, it just doesn't matter—what happens to stock prices today doesn't unduly affect what will happen to them tomorrow. In fact, the future price of a stock is no more predictable than the random occurrence of a different number in a series. Random walk theorists also believe that the market is such an efficient place that every single piece of news or data that could be used to make an investment decision is already discounted in the price of the stock. I think this is hokum. All information is *not* immediately discounted by the marketplace. The markets are not at all efficient. Any time greed and fear rule, efficiency loses. We'll discuss, in the rest of this book, the fundamental, technical, and psychological indicators that give us the winning edge. Place absolute faith in none of them, but use all of them to see the big picture.

You let the random walkers walk. You're a runner. They can chat about the merits of their various beliefs and theories while they *walk* around the track. When they finally reach the finish line, they'll find that you've long since copped the gold and are now relaxing in the hot tub you purchased while they were patting themselves on the back about their theory. Bernard Baruch and J. Paul Getty didn't believe in random walk. Among some of the most respected contemporary investment analysts, Warren Buffett, John Templeton, Albert Nicholas, and Michael Price must not believe in random walk. Why not? Take a look at their long-term investment records versus the stock market and you'll find out. In short, let the random walkers walk at random. You run—don't walk. And you run with a goal in mind— bringing home the gold.

CHAPTER 9

PEAK PERFORMANCE AND OFF DAYS

Even the Best Competitors Have Both

This may be the shortest chapter in the book, but it's one of the most important. Its message is that you must expect the occasional loss, often due to factors beyond your control. When that happens, you have to get up, dust yourself off, and get back into the race. Only those who don't get up are losers.

October 19, 1987, is a day that will be long remembered—and not fondly—by virtually everyone who was an active investor during what had been, until August of that year, a ripsnorting bull market. Virtually all of us, contrarians as well as those in the pack, went running like lemmings into the abyss that day. (It's amazing, though, that if you read their ad copy today, you'll find that 106 percent of all market-letter writers predicted the crash *to the hour*.) Just prior to October 19, I was engaged in a relatively conservative index option straddle-writing program (or at least as conservative as one can be when one writes straddles). I had written options so far out of the money that only a catastrophic, unprecedented market that moved some 800 points in a week of trading could jeopardize my positions. In fact, as we all now know, that is precisely what happened. The handwriting was on the wall on Friday, October 16, when the market fell 108 points, which was the biggest one-day decline in the history of the stock market. At that point, I had relatively small losses but decided that I had already stayed too long at the fair.

How had I gotten into this mess? Simple. We investment professionals have sophisticated and highly technical terminology for such situations. We call it a "boo-boo"—or, if anyone's listening, an "error in judgment." Similarly, we have a term for where I would have been financially if I hadn't taken immediate action—"in deep kimchee."

Recognizing this, I entered market orders to buy back all my option positions at the opening bell on Monday morning. Little did I know. Even though I made the right move in deciding to cut my losses by covering on Monday morning, by the time the Chicago Board Options Exchange opened the Index Options on Monday, the securities underlying the index had already been plummeting for two hours. As a result, even my market orders on the opening rotation cost me the proverbial arm and leg. It could have been worse, of course. Had I not made the decision on Friday to sell on Monday morning, I might have been faced with that decision at midday or at the end of the day on Monday, when my brokerage firm realized that it was in their best interest to close out the positions for me. Had that happened, I would have lost three times as much in that single day as I did. And, in fact, I've made a good deal of my money back in the ensuing months. There's a highly technical term for this phenomenon, too—we call it "good luck."

The point of recounting this painful personal experience is to remind you that we—*all of us*—do have good days and bad days in the market. Just as there are days when athletes can do no wrong—when they pull on inner reserves they didn't realize they had, the track is just right, the weather is perfect, their personal lives are in order, and they walk into the arena knowing that this is their day. There are, of course, days when, for no apparent reason, an athlete just can't seem to put it together. The commentators in the booth say, "Looks like so and so is having an off day, Jim." In sports, we expect off days as part of the game. You must develop the same expectation in the investment game. If you dwell on your occasional off days, sooner or later your performance will be affected and your ability to pull away from the pack will be hindered.

There are really two lessons to be learned here. One is that off days are an inevitable part of the investing game. You'll have your share of successes, and you'll fall short of investment success from time to time. Accept your losses with equanimity. Again, only liars and revisionist historians come in first every single time they compete and in every single event. The idea, as we'll discuss in the rest of this book, is to do so well on those days and in those events in which we excel that our failures become merely an opportunity to learn lessons that will allow us to be even more successful the next time out. Remember, Babe Ruth and Hank Aaron hit more home runs than any other baseball players in history; along the way in pursuit of that goal, they also struck out more times than almost anyone else. There's no shame, and, if you learn from your mistakes and strictly limit your losses, there's no long-term financial setback in sustaining the occasional loss.

The other important lesson to be learned here is that, when all indicators tell you that it's time to pull away from the pack, do it. From April to August of 1987, a remarkably steady stream of unparalleled optimism issued forth from every financial expert in *The Wall Street Journal,* on the Financial News Network, in the various investment newsletters, on "Wall Street Week," and at the local corner deli. Everybody in America thought it was a piece of cake to make money in the market. That universal optimism in itself was a screaming 250-decibel warning to get out of the market. So why didn't those of us who think we're pretty savvy follow our own indicators? Well, every now and then we all get caught up in the euphoria and the excitement.

I was a paratrooper in the army. For the most part, I had the good sense to respect the awesome forces of nature around me. (There is nothing like hurtling toward the earth at 125 m.p.h. to remind you what gravity is all about.) Yet, every now and then, for just a brief shining moment, I actually felt as if I could fly. For that moment I felt that I had "slipped the surly bonds of earth" and wasn't subject to the same physical laws that constrained everyone else. Fortunately, those moments never lasted long enough to cover the distance from the airplane to the ground. I always found the ripcord. By analogy, that's what happened to a lot of us during the third quarter and the early part of the fourth quarter of 1987. We actually believed that Newton's laws of motion had been suspended as far as the market was concerned and that 3600 was just around the corner. The market was kind enough to remind us that this was not the case.

The crucial lesson is that when the stock market is doing so well that it seems as if things can't get any better, they can't. And they won't. And if we think we can fly without wings, we're bound to find out that we can't. It may someday be done, but to the best of my knowledge, it hasn't been done yet.

Now what happens if, even having read all this, it does happen to you? Cut your losses, competitors, and press on. Babe Ruth and Hank Aaron didn't hit those home runs by thinking of quitting every time they struck out. Roger Bannister didn't break through the four-minute-mile barrier on his first attempt. He ran hundreds, possibly thousands, of time before he succeeded. Would you consider all those previous attempts failures? Of course not! In the game of investing, you don't have to be a John Walker (who has now run the mile in less than four minutes more than 100 times) or a Jesse Owens (who broke six world records at the 1936 Olympics) or break 14 world records in various events (as Paavo Nurmi did in the 1920s). So don't despair if you don't set a record of your own in investing the first time out. As long as you can survey your actions honestly and learn from your mistakes, investment success will eventually be yours.

The primary difference between success in the athletic decathlon and success in the investing decathlon is that, in the latter, as long as your mind is clear, you can succeed. The athletic decathlon is primarily for the young. The investing decathlon is for the smart. The wonderful thing about it is that it can be played for an entire lifetime. Most of us begin to acquire the means to invest sometime in our 20s. Assuming that sometime in our 70s, 80s or 90s, we decide to slow down, that's still 50 or 60 or 70 years of fun and games.

With that in mind, let's select our events.

CHAPTER 10

RUNNING WITH THE PACK

Long Shots—Why Bother?

In any sport, a time may come when you are so far down in total points needed that you choose to take greater risk in order to make up your deficit. While you know in advance that you will probably stumble, you may be at a point in the competition where you are so far out of it that you decide the risk is worth taking. You do so recognizing that you may sustain an injury as, in attempting to catch up, you stretch yourself beyond your body's limits. You'll be tempted to do this in your investing, as well. I have one word of advice for you: Don't.

In investing, *unlike* the decathlon or any other sport, if you're down, most often the best way to move back up is slowly and steadily. Even if you *haven't* lost, the best way to move up is slowly and steadily. Too many of us are tempted to take the 100-to-1 shots just for the fun of it. Because of that, we need to discuss them.

I do not recommend the investment strategies described in this chapter. They are *less* likely to return 10 to 1 than the strategies we'll discuss in later chapters. As for that fabled 100-to-1 shot, it comes along so seldom that it's better to do all the right things in your investing, *expecting* a 3-to-1 return and being increasingly pleased and surprised when it goes better. It's sort of like looking for a pot of gold at the base of every rainbow. If you look at enough rainbows, sooner or later you may discover a gold nugget or two worth tens of thousands of dollars; but spending the same amount of time *mining* for gold would have produced far more.

Should you choose to ignore this advice and should you actually make money in spite of yourself, for heaven's sake, ascribe it to what it is—lucky timing. If you believe that you struck this pay dirt through skill or superior analysis or clever research, whatever you made through sheer luck on this one you'll give back dozens, scores, or hundreds of times over. As John Kenneth Galbraith once said, "Financial genius consists almost entirely of a well-developed capacity for self-delusion combined with a rising market."

Does this mean that 100-to-1 shots don't exist? No, it doesn't. But you are better off looking to make reasonable rates of return on your money in the investments we cover in the following chapters and accept the idea that, if you apply intelligent and reasonable investing principles, and if you are lucky (and have been very, very good all year long) every now and then Santa will bring you one of these 100-to-1 gems.

Far better to take reasonable risks and expect a reasonable return and acknowledge that anything more is just icing on the cake. You'd be surprised how often, by devoting your attention to the 10 "events" discussed in the two chapters following this one, that you'll get all that extra icing. With that in mind, let's take a look at some of these areas which offer so much glowing hope and so little substance. Since, for the most part, the fake jewels listed below also carry the highest commission to those who sell them, you'll be hearing a great deal about them in your investing lifetime.

NEW ISSUES

Let's start at the beginning: most new issues aren't worth buying. We said earlier that, if it truly is a hot issue (that is, if the underwriters have given it an offering price below the one that investors feel reflects its value), you probably won't get any of it anyway. What's left are all the new issues that investors with much greater financial wherewithal and much greater clout with their broker have already rejected. And don't believe the line that most brokers will hand you, that you are getting a bargain both because this company is the next IBM or Xerox and because you can purchase this issue with absolutely no commission (this really must be your lucky day!). Anytime someone who makes a living on commission tells you that you can buy something for no commission, you can be certain someone else is paying that commission and passing it on to you in some disguised form—usually disguised because, if you knew how much the commission amounted to, you wouldn't be dumb enough to pay it.

Whether a new issue is a brand-new company that has never before sold shares to the public or, as is more likely in poor markets, is simply a new equity or bond offering of an existing company, the pattern is the same. Bright young investment bankers will get on the nationwide "squawk box" or on the firm's national wire system and extoll ad infinitum and ad nauseam the sometimes questionable virtues of the company. Next comes the full-court press by the branch sales manager. Let's say the stock is priced to sell at $16 with "no commission" to you. In fact, had you purchased another stock selling on one of the exchanges for $12, the commission at a discount broker would have been $40 or $45 for 100 shares and, even at a full-commission firm, would probably have been no more than $60 to $80. Because the underwriters are paying the broker's commission, however, the commission you never see might instead be, let's say, $1 per share, or $100. There is, of course, nothing to prevent the firm or the branch manager from tacking on an additional 10 cents or 20 cents in commission. And this is precisely what usually happens when the offering is a dog.

If it doesn't sell, the brokerage firms involved, rather than lowering the price, usually simply increase the commission. It's very easy for the individual stockbroker to rationalize that he or she is still doing you a service. After all, didn't the broker's investment bankers say that it was a great deal? And besides, the broker just gave you a winner last week, so even if this one doesn't work out, you're still okay and he or she is $100 or $120 better off for every 100 shares you buy. Unlike already-traded securities, which, if you buy in greater quantity, often carry a lower commission as a percentage of the total, new issues pay a fixed commission regardless of the number of shares sold. That is, using the same example as above, 1,000 shares of a publicly traded stock selling at $12 might cost you, say $100 to $140 or so at a discount broker and probably between $200 and $300 at a full-commission firm. If, however, your broker sells you 1,000 shares of this new issue, he or she receives the full $1 (or $1.20) on *each* share. Can you blame the broker for getting all fired up about some of these (non-)issues? Which would you rather sell, something that gives you a $300 commission or something that gives you a $1,000 commission? The best advice we can give regarding new issues is that *if* we are in a raging bull market and *if* your broker is one of those ethical souls in the industry and *if* he or she would like to continue doing business with you, then you *might* be okay buying the occasional new issue.

SPECIAL OFFERINGS

Another endeavor in which the stockbroker makes an inordinately large commission is the area of "special offerings." If you deal with a full-commission brokerage firm for any length of time, sooner or later you'll get an excited call from your broker telling you that such-and-such a company insider or group of insiders or major institution has decided, for tax or legal or some other spurious reason, to sell a significant block of its securities and (can you believe your luck?) you are one of the chosen few who has an opportunity to purchase some of this stock. If you really believe that sophisticated corporate or investing insiders and professionals are selling shares of this company even though they don't want to and *you* are one of the chosen who get to profit from their misfortune, you don't need this book. You need, instead, to do two things. First, you need to take all your investable funds and find a responsible investment counselor. There is no way you should be investing your own money. Second, you should have your head examined. Nobody does you any favors in this arena. They are jostling for position with the other competitors and there's nobody who is going to say, "Oh, please step right out in front of me." The real benefit of "special offerings" is that you can often identify great short-sale candidates from among this group.

OPTIONS

There is a third area where brokers receive an inordinate amount of commission revenue: the options market. It's not that the commissions themselves are so onerous, it's just that the price of option trading is eternal vigilance and constant churning. Now, please don't mistake this kind of churning with the illegal activity the New York Stock Exchange punishes brokers for doing when they, usually without the customer's consent, overtrade the account. Oh, no! In the options market, we've eliminated the middleman; options customers mercilessly churn *themselves* without any assistance from the stockbroker. Let's talk about two long-shot plays: buying stock and index options and writing naked stock and index options.

Do people make any money buying options? Hardly ever. So why do they do it, you ask? Because, like the guy hitting himself in the head with hammer, it feels so good when they stop? No, it's because that old ham actor, *100-to-1* is always waiting in the wings. Can you hit one of these 100-to-1 shots? Sure—with roughly the same probability that lightning will strike nearby when you have your camera ready and the lens cap off: it doesn't happen often, but when it does, it's big enough news that everyone notices. Forget right now the gobbledygook that you've heard that you "limit your risk" when you buy options. While it is true that, if you buy a company at $50 and it declines to zero on every 100 shares, you lose $5,000. If, instead, you had bought a call on that company for $5, you would have lost only $500. But I'm convinced that, rather than sit on the sidelines, most people try to make it back and would take the next $500 loss and the next and the next. It is far more likely that you will lose 100 percent of your capital every time out in options than in common stocks. The net effect is the same: if a company is going to go to zero, you can lose $5,000 over time or you can play the options market and lose it faster. Limited risk? Sure it's limited—to every nickel you put in. To those who respond, "Yeah? Well, I'm making money in options right now," I reply, "That's great. Enjoy it while you can." Over the last 20 years I've seen thousands of people play the options market. For the most part, the *sad* thing is that they're successful in the short term. If only they'd lose everything all at once, they'd think twice about sticking with options. Unfortunately, many of them do make a few hundred or a few thousand dollars before the roof caves in. In 20 years, I have yet to see a *single* investor consistently make money buying options.

Nor do I think much of "put protection." The idea of the

put-protection strategy is that you buy a stock you think is going to go up in value and at the same time buy a put option on the underlying security. The put is supposed to function as a sort of insurance policy against any decline in the price of the stock for as long as you own the option. Of course, you could do the same thing using "call protection" when you sell short. You sell the stock short and simultaneously buy a call option on the underlying security. The call option is supposed to insure you against a rise in the price of the stock. Most of the projections advocating this strategy leave out the effect of brokerage commissions. For my money, I can get the same effect by simply placing a stop order. If I buy a stock for $40, there's nothing to prevent me from putting in a "sell stop" at $37. I buy the company's stock believing it will go up in value. If I am wrong, however, and the stock declines, when it reaches $37, my order is automatically converted to a market order to sell. That doesn't mean that I'll be getting $37 per share. I might sell at $37, $36¾, or $37⅛, but I will sell at somewhere around $37. I can gain the same protection by putting a "buy stop" above my short sale. The difference between simply putting in a sell stop or a buy stop and using call protection or put protection is that, when you put in a buy stop or a sell stop, your broker doesn't receive any immediate commission. Should this position be sold out (or bought back, in the case of a short sale), the broker will receive that commission, but that's no more than he or she would have received when you wound the position down, anyway. With call protection or put protection, however, the broker gets a commission on your purchase or sale of the underlying security as well as on your purchase of the put or call. But, as the TV ad says, "Wait! There's more!" Assuming that you've purchased a six-month or nine-month put or call, in order to continue your "protection" you get to lay out more cash for more insurance protection when that option expires. Three guesses who gets the commission when you lay on this new "protection."

Can you, with the aid of sophisticated computer programs and expert advice, fully hedge the risks of securities investing by using options? Sure. The problem is that, when all is said and done, by removing the risk, you remove the reward. You've spent so much money futzing around with all this silly stuff that you would have been better off putting your money in Treasury bills.. Then, instead of devising all these clever little systems, you could have used your brain for something worthwhile—like determining the primary trend of the market you are in.

If you think buying options is dumb, writing naked options is usually dumber. Remember that an option position is considered uncovered (naked) when you write an option without owning the underlying security. You don't *own* anything to deliver when someone says, "Okay, you sold me the option. Now I am exercising it. Where's my stock?" As Daniel Drew, one of the great bear raiders of a bygone era, said,

> He who sells what isn't his'n
> Must buy it back or go to prison.

Drew was referring to short selling at the time. Naked options are far more dangerous. We *can* control, via stop orders, much of the risk in short selling. In the case of writing naked options, your potential loss is unlimited. (That's right—100 percent of everything you invested plus 100 percent of your house, car, and future earnings.) You can—theoretically—lose more than you put up when selling short, but when you write naked options, you can face unlimited catastrophe *faster* and with far greater likelihood. The only exception here is when you write naked puts on stocks. *Never do this with index options!* When you write a naked put on a stock, the worst that can happen is that the stock could be "put" to you. If you were going to buy it, anyway, you might buy it *and* get the premium income for writing the put.

If the above option "investments" have one thing in common, it is that the action in all of them is so intense that we feel that, if we don't take action this very second, such an opportunity will never rise again. Options are simply so volatile that it's easy to forget we are playing with real money. If you must play the options market, please remember my earlier suggestion and pay for each purchase with real cash dollars.

In the case of new issues and special offerings, it's the broker, rather than the volatility of the market, that is telling you this is the opportunity of a lifetime. Funny thing about these "opportunities of a lifetime"—they seem to come around with remarkable frequency. Like the aforementioned streetcars, the truth is, if you wait 25 minutes or so, another will come along. Don't ever rush into any investment without carefully thinking it through. Remember, *better you should be left standing at the dock than be the last passenger to board the Titanic.*

PENNY STOCKS

"Penny" stocks are certainly among the other long shots we should talk about. Can you make money buying penny stocks? Of course you can, just as you can win a race by walking on your hands, but it isn't very likely. Again, over-the-counter penny stocks trade with such astronomical markups between the bid and asked prices that the people who sell them to you are making some very serious dollars. The problem is compounded because now even more middlemen are involved. In addition to the salesperson making a fine markup by buying on the "inside offer" and selling to you at the asked price or higher, the OTC securities dealer makes a profit in exchange for taking the risk of holding these stocks in inventory. As a result, you'll often see penny stocks bid 15 cents, asking 25 cents. Only a dime's worth of difference, you say? Listen—if someone's willing to pay you $1,500 for these stocks if you're selling and will sell it to you for $2,500 if you're buying, it costs you $1,000 no matter how you look at it. In these situations, everybody except you gets a piece of the pie.

This is not to say that *low-priced* stocks aren't a great way to play a bull market. But usually those selling for literally pennies a share have nowhere to go but down. Again, it's sort of like buying options. Sure, your risk is limited—to everything you put in. From 80 to 90 percent of these stocks which you buy at a dime or a quarter or a half-dollar usually go to a penny, two pennies, or three pennies, where they languish until they declare bankruptcy. Of course, there are the occasional brilliant finds in the penny stock market. But for every one of those I can show you 40 or 50 that went belly up and another 50 or 60 that, while they may not be bankrupt, have never done anything. This is like playing Russian roulette with two revolvers, one

pointed at each temple—and one of them has a full load. Want
bargains? Look at some of the New York Stock Exchange listed
issues selling for $5 or $10 at the bottom of the next bear
market. Don't waste your time making the penny stock houses
rich. They don't call them Churnum, Burnum, Blindem, and
Robbem, Inc., for nothing.

FADS

There are two other investing areas which, while not quite so
egregious as those discussed above, will provide mediocre results, in my opinion. The first of these is buying the latest hot
fad. That's not to say that you can't make a significant amount
of money buying shares in a nationwide chain of yogurt shops
and television home-shopping services. As a matter of fact, if
you apply the standards of value we'll discuss later and you
discover one of these types of companies early on, you can make
some very good money. The problem with all such fads is that
usually only one or two companies define the parameters of their
particular market. In other words, if you discover these yogurt
shops or one of these television shopping services long before
everyone else begins to think they are great, you can get a very
worthwhile ride. In that case, you're buying a chance on something you have thought about and decided is a good opportunity.
When everyone in America has already jumped on the band-
wagon and there are now 15 or 20 such companies all clamoring
for a finite market, it's insane to jump in and hope that a me-too
company, which lacks the entrepreneurial drive and innovation
of the original market leader, will perform as well either as a
company or as an investment for you. Every now and then, one
of these outfits will ride on the coattails of another successful
company, but it doesn't happen often. And very often, even the
original company in the arena will have a meteoric rise and then
crash and burn. It's sort of like a runner who makes his or her
move too soon, peaks early, and stumbles into the dust. I mean,
was it really reasonable to expect that a nation in love with
automobiles and shopping malls was going to give up both over-
night so that they could sit glued in glorious isolation in front of

the idiot box and buy everything from abacuses to zoot suits? It's amazing what some people, swept up in the madness of the crowd, will believe—and equally amazing how a little common sense is all it takes to see through all this and be a successful investor. Avoid fads. You'll have plenty of opportunity to buy quality companies (with real products and services) that have fallen, temporarily, on hard times. As we'll soon see, that's where the real money is.

"BUY AND HOLD"

The other strategy I am going to caution you about is something many money managers will tell you to do; they'll advise "the small investor" (read: anyone who isn't an institution) to buy and hold. I don't believe in the buy and hold strategy. I *do* believe in long-term investing. There's a difference.

There are always some securities that run contracyclical to the major market trends, and I am willing to hold onto them through good markets and bad because there is something about them that allows them to rise in value even while all other stocks are taking a beating. But, for the most part, when I say "long term" I refer to the duration of the primary trend. In the case of the great secular bull markets, the primary uptrend might cover a great deal of time. In the 20s, it lasted for eight years, from 1921 to 1929. After World War II it lasted for 16 years, from 1949 to 1965. That may not be buy-and-hold time, but it's definitely *very* long term. By the same token, there were long dry spells from 1930 to 1949 and from 1965 to 1981. That doesn't mean that there weren't good investing opportunities on the up- and downside during those times. It simply means that, in the first two instances, for the *most* part, *most* stocks rose in value for that entire time period. For the *most* part, *most* stocks in the second two time frames lost value or appreciated only very little. I don't confuse long-term investing with a buy-and-hold strategy. Neither should you. Buy and hold, for most people, is simply another way of not having to face up to the decision when it's time to sell a security.

Most of us with any experience in the market have agonized

over a stock purchase, done extensive research, and looked for others' opinions before purchasing a stock. Yet when the signs indicate that it's time to sell, we have rationalized that somehow this one stock will resist the inevitable avalanche of selling that a bear market brings on. It's like believing that, with 500,000 tons of snow rushing down the hillside, everyone else is going to get swept away, but we are going to be left standing. And besides, since many of the "experts" tell us that we can't time the market and therefore stock selection is all that counts, we figure we are in pretty good company. Remember, institutional money managers, for the most part, are just too big to get in and out easily. Plus, as you recall, if they don't keep 80 or 90 percent of their funds invested at all times, the people who have entrusted them with their money begin to wonder what they are paying them for. Many investors, however, are happy to pay a money manager to sit on cash. As a matter of fact, one of the few stocks that actually went up on Black Monday in 1987 was a closed-end fund called GSO Trust. The manager of this fund, Charles Allmon, has been in the market for a number of years and was in roughly 80 percent cash on that day. Many investors, by purchasing shares in his fund, hired Allmon to manage part of their money. They could fire him at any time by selling their shares. But as long as they'd made the decision that they wanted him to manage their money, they didn't grouse that he chose to put it in cash.

In addition to being willing to hold *some* stocks, I am willing to hold *some* mutual funds through all kinds of markets. The *Forbes* honor roll, listing those mutual funds that do well in good markets and bad, is a good place to find funds that you may wish to buy for the long term. For the most part, you are still going to be better off selling even a good fund and putting the money to work in an interest-bearing account or selling short while the market is plummeting. It takes not only gifted management but a heck of a lot of luck to beat the 6, 10, or 14 percent you are getting on your short-term investment in money market funds while the market is falling 20 percent per year. Remember, when you buy a stock listed on an exchange or over the counter, the company itself doesn't benefit at all. The company got all their money when they originally went public. They are out of it now. For this reason, there's no need to fall in love with a company. You can still love the company—just be willing to sell its stock when it's appropriate to do so.

I think that about covers it for most of the long shots. Choosing to invest in these areas is like starting a race fifty paces back when everyone else started at the mark. You might, through superior effort, greater talent, and a whole lot of luck not only catch the pack but surpass them—but why handicap yourself needlessly?

Now that we've talked about some of the events in which we would *not* want to participate, let's move on to the 10 events we've chosen for our own investing decathlon.

CHAPTER 11

PULLING AWAY: FIVE EVENTS WE MUST BE VERY GOOD AT

In an athletic decathlon, the idea isn't to set world records in each of the 10 events. What's required is to be pretty darn good in *all* the events and to score very big in the few that you're best at—to deliver all-around fine performance along with the occasional stellar success. Completeness counts. Doing well enough to remain a competitor no matter what the event, and throwing the javelin farther than anyone else ever has or hurling our bodies farther or faster than ever before every now and again—that's the winning combination. It's the same in the stock market. Consistency is the key: if you're a competitor across the board, you'll have your occasional record breaker but won't give it all back in down markets.

In our investing decathlon, I have singled out 10 events. Five of them are in this chapter. These are "investing events" at which you must be very good. You've got to understand what they are and when to use them. You may use these five once in a year or once in a decade, depending upon your own personal circumstances. In the next chapter, we'll talk about the remaining five—the ones which you must *master,* for those are the ones with the biggest chance for truly exceptional performance. But you must be all-around good in all 10. Let's build a foundation with the first five, then pull away from the pack with the next five. That's the winning ticket—that's when you succeed in bringing home the gold.

The five events in which we want to become very good are:

1. Buying and selling income instruments.
2. Writing covered calls and uncovered puts.
3. Buying and selling popular stocks.

4. Knowing when to "pyramid" and when to "dollar–cost average."
5. Buying and selling precious metals.

The five events that we must master, which round out our investing decathlon, are:

6. Buying and selling the common stocks that, today, nobody else wants.
7. Buying, selling and hedging with convertible bonds and preferreds.
8. Selling short.
9. Buying and selling warrants, SCOREs, "long-term" options, and IPs.
10. Buying, selling, and switching growth and total-return mutual funds and closed-end funds.

In this chapter we'll look at those at which we need to be very good. In the following chapter we'll consider the five events that we must master.

BUYING AND SELLING INCOME INSTRUMENTS

As you recall from earlier chapters, a number of investment vehicles are available to us if we are interested in maximizing the income we receive from our investments rather than purchasing them in anticipation of (capital) gain. These include: U.S. government obligations like Treasury bills, Treasury notes, and Treasury bonds; the various U.S. government agencies' debt obligations; municipal bonds, be they general obligation or revenue bonds; bonds issued by corporations; bonds issued by corporations that are convertible into shares of the underlying common stock; income mutual funds, both open-end and closed-end; zero coupon bonds; and money market funds, both taxable and tax-free. Many would also include the common stock of utility issues in this category. I don't because I view these as common stock that may or may not be a good purchase from a total-return standpoint at any given time. Besides, what I'm talking about is pure income. I view the income received from owning a utility stock as icing on the cake. But the cake is still the capital gain I'm looking for in appreciation of the underlying shares of stock.

For the same reason, we'll discuss convertible bonds in the next chapter. I like convertibles and view them as a way to achieve capital gains in many companies, often at less risk than the common stock would allow. The income from the convertible bond, like a dividend on a common stock, is just icing on the cake for me.

Looking at all of these income alternatives, the two that make the most sense for our investing decathlon are money market funds and T bills. Both are easily obtained from virtually any stockbrokerage firm. Money market funds may also be purchased directly from many mutual fund companies, and T bills are available at most banks or directly from the Federal Reserve Banking System. That's not to say that there aren't excellent opportunities in government, agency, municipal, or corporate bonds or income-oriented mutual funds. But to do justice to the subject of income-producing securities, we'd need to write a whole other book. *This* book is about going up against some very strong competitors and distancing them. When we talk about bringing home the gold, we're talking about using income investments primarily as a place to park our money between capital growth opportunities.

Never forget that there is a high risk of interest rate fluctuation in income investing. While the income stream may be secure and while, upon maturity 20 or 30 years from now, the obligation will probably be paid off at full face value, there is the very real likelihood of significant roller-coaster action along the way. As a result of the prevailing inflation rate and various interest rates, on any given day the bond you purchased may trade *significantly* above or below the price you paid for it. Since I don't choose to buy and hold my other investments, as a matter of course, through thick and thin, I don't wish to do the same with income investments, either. I have no interest in being locked in to one investment when another may prove to be far superior. For this reason, government-agency, municipal, and corporate debt instruments as well as Treasury notes and Treasury bonds are most useful when your analysis leads you to believe that a deflationary period is ahead. While there are a number of sophisticated trading strategies using fixed income securities, most of us invest in fixed income for peace of mind, liquidity, and relative safety. Their value lies primarily in protecting your hard-earned gold, rather than in bringing it home.

Zero coupon bonds, which pay no interest from year to year but are sold at very steep discounts to face value and are redeemed at face value upon maturity, may have a place in some portfolios. For instance, if you choose to speculate with most of your funds but want the certainty of having money available to you down the road, you might place some of your available funds in zero coupon bonds. For the most part, these are worthwhile only in an IRA, Keogh, or other tax-deferred account. The reason for this is that, even though the bonds pay no interest, the Internal Revenue Service, in its infinite wisdom, has decided to tax you as if you received the income. There are, however, certain issues that were available before the IRS made this decision and are therefore "grandfathered." These don't mature until well after the year 2000 but can be purchased for roughly 10 cents on the dollar. What this means is that, if you are an investor 40 years old who wants to speculate in the marketplace and has $50,000 to risk, you might place $10,000 of it into one of these issues. In that way, upon maturity 25 years from now, your $10,000 will return $100,000 to you. (Of course, with inflation, the $100,000 might very well buy no more than $10,000 does today.) Meanwhile, you could take the other $40,000 and attempt to make serious money with it.

You can overcome the problem of being locked in to your income investment by buying an income-oriented mutual fund. If you buy a closed-end fund, however, and you are going to park money for only a short time, you have the double whammy of being subject to interest rate fluctuations and having to pay two commissions to get in and out. If you decide to park funds in an open-end mutual fund, you may be subject to loads, redemption fees, or 12b-1 fees. Even if you get into a truly no-load mutual fund, you are still subject to the vagaries of the bond market. That is, if you decide to redeem your shares in four or six months when interest rates have gone higher and bond prices have therefore gone down, you may still sell at a loss.

That's why, for our purposes, we are primarily interested in T bills and money market funds. You can purchase both from virtually any stockbroker, full-commission or discount, or you may purchase them directly. Money market funds may be purchased directly from a number of mutual fund families and, as we'll see in the next chapter, many investors take advantage of the mutual fund family's "telephone switch" privileges to take money out of the market and put it in that fund family's money market fund for varying periods of time.

You may also purchase T bills directly through commercial banks or the Federal Reserve Bank's regional offices. I personally find it far more convenient to buy through my brokerage firm. It's important that you become familiar with both these vehicles in order to be able to park funds when none of the recommended investment events outlined in the next chapter offer you a worthwhile place to invest funds at a certain point in time.

The final income-oriented investment is for those investors who must maximize their dividend income but who can still accept some market risk. You recall, from our previous discussion of PRIMEs and SCOREs, that PRIMEs give their holders all the dividend income as well as some participation in the up-side potential of the underlying stock. For this reason, PRIMEs cost less than the common they are derived from, yield more, and, assuming that a dividend continues to be paid, have an "investment floor." That is, *as long as they pay some dividend that is perceived as secure,* they will not go below the price at which their dividend yield is equivalent to the best returns investors can find anywhere else by buying debt securities like bonds. While I personally much prefer the meteoric potential of SCOREs and am willing to assume the risks inherent in them, PRIMEs may be better for some portfolios. One time to use PRIMEs is when we believe there will be an extended period of sideways motion in the markets. Another is when we think a major bottom is approaching and we are beginning to nibble at the more exciting opportunities but want to put the bulk of our capital into depressed blue chips and keep a solid income stream.

WRITING COVERED CALLS AND
UNCOVERED PUTS

The writing of covered options is another area in which you should be willing to compete. There will be times when you purchase a security that enjoys a great deal of appreciation. If you are genuinely on the fence about selling it and unsure of which direction the market is going in, one of the strategies you might use is to write an option against your position. For example, let's say that you've bought a stock at 22 that has run up to $40 per share. The experts are giving you no clear reverse-indicator signals as to the direction of the market. Half of them are forecasting a decline, while half of them see the market continuing to roar ahead. (If *all* of them thought it was going to roar ahead, this would be your sell signal. You're on the fence because they're not.) Perhaps all the other fundamental, technical, and psychological indicators you review also leave you befuddled. That's okay. There will be times like that. What you might do, in this case, is write an option that gives you $300 in premium income. This way, should the stock decline, you've at least received $300 in income from writing the option. If, however, the stock stays right around where it is, you continue to own it and you've received the extra $300 for writing the option. If the stock does continue its rise, at least you've gotten an extra $300 out of it. Assuming that you wrote a call with a strike price of $40, you effectively sell at $43, and leave the rest to the person who purchased the option from you. Is all this worth it? Occasionally. Writing covered options is a technique to use when we're not in a bull market or a bear market, but a crab market. (I call any market that moves sideways for any length of time a crab market. This is not simply because crabs move sideways, but because people, deprived of their daily dose of market action, tend to get pretty crabby during these periods.) You need one event to perfect for the occasional crab market. This is it.

There are also many investors who purchase stocks and sell an option against that position at the same time. These are competitors who are happy to maximize their return by being on the house side of this particular casino. They purchase the aforementioned stock at $40 and immediately write a $40 call option against it. The only time I can see doing this is when stocks are so low that I don't expect much of a further decline for them but I don't see a good upward move starting yet. If I see a great deal of up-side potential, I'm not about to give all that up by writing an option. Covered option writers are like the people who buy PRIMEs rather than SCOREs. They're happy with a small but relatively steady return. The problem with this strategy is that they are not protected against serious declines in the underlying common stock.

There are some ways to increase this return *and* reduce our risk at the same time. The Securities and Exchange Commission has elected rather a broad interpretation of what a covered option is. The underlying common stock is but one way of securing the option position. Other ways include convertible bonds, convertible preferreds, warrants, and buying options (to create a spread). While greater leverage can be gained by using these other securities instead of the common stock, again, if I've purchased the convertible bond or convertible preferred or warrant, it's because I believe they will go up in value. If I believe that, why would I write an option against it and effectively give up what will probably be the biggest percentage of the gain I've been expecting? Nonetheless, by using, say, the convertible bond to secure the position, we can get greater interest income and if we have to convert the bond into common stock to meet our obligation to the option buyer, we still "lock in" the price we effectively pay for the common, so it behooves us to be familiar with the writing of covered options. As in all other investment endeavors, the best way to learn is to practice with play money first, and then actually do it. You may find that, while the rewards are relatively low, so are the risks. If you're happy with a good—never great—return year in and year out, writing covered options—especially using convertible bonds or preferreds, which offer greater income than the underlying common stock—may be for you.

Writing uncovered puts is a strategy best used when we believe that a stock we've been following is somewhere near the range in which we'd like to buy it, but recognize that it may decline more. The idea is that, if a stock we'd like to own is selling at $22 per share, we probably wouldn't mind paying $19 a share for it, so we'd do as follows:

A stock selling at $22 per share would certainly have strike prices of $20 as well as $25. If we'd really like to buy the stock, we might sell (write) the $25 put. For an option with an expiration only a couple months out, there'd probably be very little premium. The $25 option might fetch only 3½ points, or $350. We'd pay $2200 to buy the stock outright ($22 per share times 100 shares). By writing the put, we receive $350 in premium income and, if the stock is "put" to us at $25, we pay $2500 for it ($25 per share times 100 shares) but, since we received $350 in premium income, our real cost for the 100 shares is $2150. This is the *worst* that could happen. Should the stock close at $25 or higher on expiration date, we take the $350 premium and pocket it with no obligation whatsoever. We've made $350 on zero dollars invested—not a bad percentage rate of return.

To return to our statement that we'd actually prefer owning the stock at $19 per share—we'd need a slightly different strategy. Instead of writing an uncovered $25 put, we'd write the $20 put. Assuming the premium here was 1 point, or $100, we'd only pocket $100 if the stock never went below $20 per share and thus wasn't put to us. If, on the other hand, it declined to any point below $20, it *would* be put to us. Let's say it went to 19½ per share. It would be put to us at $20, or $2000 for 100 shares. We'd pay $2000, less the $100 we received as a premium, or $1900 for a stock then selling for $1950—and which we were perfectly willing to own at $2200, the price we would have paid had we purchased it outright rather than writing the put.

Is it worth the extra effort to do all this? Often it is. Especially in a sideways market. If the stocks go down and get put to us, well, we wanted to own them, anyway. And if they don't decline, we keep collecting the premium income. It's nice to be on the house's side!

BUYING AND SELLING POPULAR STOCKS

Our next event of interest is buying and selling stocks that everyone else already wants. Normally, there's not much sense in buying these. If a stock I'm looking at is in 50 or 100 different mutual funds' portfolios, the market's been rising for a number of months or even years, and the stock sports a hefty price-earnings ratio in the high teens or above, I need to face the fact that I'm probably too late to enjoy the lion's share of the move in this one. Nonetheless, since I know that sometimes these little scuppers look so good that we just can't resist, they're worth talking about.

There *are* times when it's okay to jump aboard an already-moving train. If you simply didn't have the capital at the market bottom but you use all the indicators we discuss and are convinced that that *was* the bottom and you now do have the capital, welcome aboard. Don't be priggish about this: if the stock and the industry group are moving smartly ahead and you didn't get the absolute bottom but you don't believe the market is anywhere near an absolute top, it's okay to go for a ride. As an example, if a stock sold nine months ago at $24 and the market's moving ahead and, as a result, this stock is now $36, but all our indicators point to continued up side for the market and the industry, you may buy a stock that no one loved at $24 and everyone loves at $36. Just be aware that you are $12 closer to that point ($48? $60? who knows?) at which nobody will love the market or the industry and the stock will enter a period of cyclical decline.

To get a real sense of the cyclicality of individual issues and a somewhat different point of view on buying popular stocks, pick up a copy of Stan Weinstein's *Secrets for Profiting in Bull and Bear Markets*. Stan discusses in great detail his notion of the progression of stocks through various stages in their cycle. Stage 1 is the basing area, stage 2 the advancing stage, stage 3 the top area, and stage 4 the declining phase. He argues that, while investors may try to buy in the basing area, they're usually better off buying after the stock has already begun moving up.

Differences in strategy are what makes stock markets and ball games. For my part, I'd just as soon buy early on—when nobody else is bidding the price up.

And remember that these comments regarding buying after the rise is already evident don't apply when the market in general is already overheated to the point where you believe most of the move has already happened. How will you know when this occurs? Well, we'll talk about timing the market in Chapter 13.

One final comment on buying stocks when everyone's already in love with the market. When everything in a particular industry is moving up except one issue, don't think you're being smart to buy the one that hasn't yet moved. You're not the only competitor in this event; as a matter of fact, it's a very crowded field. If the stock hasn't moved while all its peers have, there's a reason.

PYRAMIDING AND DOLLAR-COST AVERAGING

The next event in which we must be good enough to compete is in "dollar-cost averaging" and its flip side, "pyramiding." These are two "systems" often advanced by various investing gurus as surefire ways to beat the market. As systems, I think both are a bunch of malarkey. That's not to say that there may not be a time when you choose to use one or the other of these techniques, but as "systems" to be relied on to take the thinking out of this business? Nonsense! This is a mental game and, as such, requires constant observation and a willingness to change strategies or even events at a moment's notice. "Systems," by whatever name they masquerade, deprive us of this flexibility by promising "autopilot" decisions.

Just what are "dollar-cost averaging" and "pyramiding"? In dollar-cost averaging, we purchase a fixed *dollar* amount of a certain stock at fixed intervals over time, regardless of the price of the stock, in order to build a portfolio. Done faithfully, this procedure reduces the *average* cost per share because more shares are purchased when the price is low—*automatically*—than when it is high. You don't guess when the low is reached. You let the market show you. *In the best of all possible worlds,* dollar-cost averaging would work something like this. We make our first purchase of 100 shares in January, when the stock is selling at $12, so we pay $1,200. It goes down so that, when we make our next purchase, in April, it's $10 a share. We buy another *120* shares because that's what $1,200 will now buy. By July, it's down to $8 and we buy another 150 shares (150 × $8 = $1,200, the fixed amount we've decided to put into this stock, come hell or high water, every quarter). By October, the stock recovers to $12, so we buy another 100, and by January the next year it's at $15. At this price $1,200 will buy only 80 shares. Finally, we buy another 80 shares in April, while it's still $15. When, in July, it's only $16, we decide it's probably not going to move much higher, so we sell our entire position. We now own the following:

---

100 shares purchased at $12 in January
120 shares purchased at $10 in April
150 shares purchased at $ 8 in July
100 shares purchased at $12 in October
 80 shares purchased at $15 in January
 80 shares purchased at $15 in April

Total   630 shares purchased altogether at an aver-
        age price of $11.43 per share ($7,200 di-
        vided by 630 shares)

Since, even if we did have the cash to buy it all at once, we'd have paid $12 per share times 630 shares, or $7,560, dollar-cost averaging seems to give us an additional $300+ worth of stock on this transaction without actually spending the $360. Now comes the sticky part. Dollar-cost averaging rests on a shaky and dangerous foundation: it *assumes* that all depressed issues will recover. The system sounds great in theory, but what happens when you buy a stock at $12 and add to your position at $10, $8, $6, and $4, only to watch it sit there for years or, worse, disappear from view altogether? Be very careful when a broker suggests you dollar-cost average some turkey he or she talked you into at a higher price. You might just be throwing good money after bad.

I have similar reservations about pyramiding. Pyramiding advocates tell us that dollar-cost averaging is all wet—that, rather than buy more shares of a stock going down, we should dump it. Any stock going down isn't worth owning; only stocks going *up* are worth owning. Therefore, proponents of this system say, we not only should dump our losers—fast—but we should *add to* our positions that are rising. If we buy a stock at $12 and it goes down, we dump. But if we buy it at $12 and it goes to $15, we buy more. At some other point, as long as it's continuing to rise, we buy more—and more and more.

Gerald Loeb, one of the first investment professionals whose works I was lucky enough to read, wrote a book in 1935 called *The Battle for Investment Survival.* In it, he advocates not averaging down, but averaging up. The stocks that he suggested we purchase more of were those which we had bought that then went up. Because most people are afraid of breaking away from the pack and exploring new ground, most investors are very uncomfortable with buying a rising security. Loeb pointed out, quite accurately, that people who would not buy a stock at $25, $30, $35, or $40 would rush in to buy if the stock then retreated to $36, thinking it was now "cheap" (down from $40). While his insights into human nature are quite telling, I can't agree with the principle of pyramiding. Pyramiding works great as long as (1) you get in early on the stock's significant rise and (2) you are in a major bull market that allows the stock to continue rising.

The problem with this is that, since you don't know whether a stock that has risen from $20 to $25 has just experienced its entire rise or is destined to reach $100, it's tough to continue putting new money in. There are times when I do this, but only when everything is lined up just so. With some securities and many mutual funds, the pendulum swings wide in both directions but always returns to the center, often on its way to the left or the right. Pyramid only when you are *convinced* that there is a 400 or 500 percent move yet ahead. It shouldn't bother us to be buying the stocks other people are starting to like now that they are moving up. Ideally, we were bright enough to buy into them when nobody liked them, but as long as the bull market is secure and as long as the industry is an essential one and as long as this company is the leader in that industry, we can add to our position along the way.

Pyramiding is a favorite of some technicians because it plays into something they desperately want to believe: that a stock in an uptrend remains in an uptrend until it violates its uptrend by beginning a downtrend. (Don't laugh—some technicians swear by this kind of tautology!)

A number of books have been written on the market, all with some variation of the title *I Made $1 Million in the Stock Market and You Can Too, So There,* that advocate pyramiding. In every case, the author has mistaken good luck and a rising market for good sense and a valid approach to investing. *Of course* this works in a rising market—what doesn't? The problem with pyramiding is that you cannibalize your own profits and get whipsawed mercilessly. What if you buy 100 shares at $12 per share and 100 shares at $15 per share and the stock goes back down to $12 per share? Well, it's not going up, so you're supposed to sell it. You break even on the lot you paid $12 a share on and lose $300 on the lot you paid $15 a share for. See? There really is one born every minute.

If I don't believe in dollar-cost averaging and pyramiding, why include them in this chapter? These are all supposed to be events we need to become good at. Remember, I said I don't like either of these techniques as "systems." As actions, however, they're fine. Let me explain. If you like a stock at $12, the fact that it goes to $8 is no reason to stop liking it. If there's some terrible reason why it's declining that leads you to believe it won't recover in a timely fashion, sell it. But if it just goes down because the market doesn't turn as fast as you thought it would and all kinds of uninformed twits are selling the stock because they're afraid of the market, then, by all means, *buy more.* Is this dollar-cost averaging? Sure. You're lowering the price you paid on your now-expanded total position.

By the same token, if the stock goes up but you still think it's a steal at $15, forget that you paid $12 for your first lot. If you think it's on its way to $30, what difference does it make that you added to your position at $15 instead of $13 or $12? Is this pyramiding? Yes. But rather than rely on some stupid system, we're relying on brainpower. The point is, every time we look at a stock, we ask ourselves, "Making the decision today—regardless of the fact that I already happen to own some of this stock at a different price—would I decide to buy it or not?" If, *today,* you'd answer yes, then buy it. If dollar-cost averaging or pyramiding is the resulting action, fine. Just don't rely on either. *Rely* on common sense.

There is one area in which I feel particularly comfortable using dollar-cost averaging. There's no guarantee that any single stock will ultimately recover and vindicate my dollar-cost averaging. There's no *guarantee* that well-chosen growth mutual funds will recover, either—but it's sufficiently likely to make me willing to put money on it or, rather, in it. If a growth mutual fund that I believe in experiences a decreasing net asset value, it may be a great opportunity to add to my position. In this manner, I dollar-cost average and end up buying shares in the fund below the "average" price at which it traded during the period in which I was buying.

Finally, it's important to be familiar with these two investing events because they are instructive in a *selling,* rather than a buying, method I like to use: "stepping out of the market" (as opposed to jumping or fleeing!). All I mean by "stepping" out of the market is that I leave it one step at a time. Very often, at market tops, the news is just so rosy and everyone is so bullish and all your friends are so enthusiastic that it's really tough to follow the indicators and sell. If you just can't bring yourself to do so, do this instead: sell half your position. If you're wrong about the market and it keeps going up, you'll still have something to talk about at your next cocktail party. *Don't buy more—* the indicators are seldom wrong, just early.

If it turns out that you should have sold everything, at least you've protected half your position—and half your capital. If everything goes okay for a while and you reach another critical juncture when you know you should sell but can't, sell half again. Pretty soon, at or near the final top, your remaining position will be so small that, when other investors are tearing out their hair and looking for good ledge space on Wall Street, you won't be married—for better or for worse—to the stock market.

BUYING AND SELLING PRECIOUS METALS

The final event at which we must be very good is investing in precious metals. There are a number of ways to invest in precious metals such as gold, silver, and platinum. We can own the physical metal itself, either by taking possession of it or by having a large U.S. or foreign bank hold it for us; we can invest in mutual funds that physically hold bullion; we can purchase coins; we can buy gold or silver mining shares; or we can invest in mutual funds that specialize in precious metals.

For my purposes, I don't believe in getting involved with any precious metals other than gold and silver. Of the two, gold is by far my favorite because I use precious metals primarily as a hedge against inflation, and gold has historically been the best hedge against inflation. A number of investment advisors talk about the role of silver as an industrial metal and the uses of platinum, palladium, and other metals. However, since an ounce of gold has historically been worth somewhere around 35 or 40 times more than an ounce of silver, it's a heck of a lot more portable, and, in case you ever have to melt it down, it's universally recognized as the ultimate store of value.

"To everything there is a season," and the season for gold is always whenever the great bulk of investors begin to fear inflation. Nowadays, gold and inflation are inextricably intertwined. Because the threat of higher inflation is an ever-present reality, I believe that we should always be ready, at the drop of a gold sovereign, to move into the precious-metals markets. Whenever inflation is temporarily "beaten," I like to buy gold. I'm not a collector, but I have some collector coins and some bullion investments that are part of my core holdings. These I won't sell unless I am convinced that the various governments of the world, starting with our own, have decided, once and for all, to stop producing paper money whenever we need to spend ourselves out of a recession. In other words, I think I'll be holding my physical gold for some time to come. This is, plain and simple, a hedge against the capriciousness of politicians. I believe the down-side risk to be quite limited and the up-side potential to be quite strong. Should you agree with my assessment, you, too, may wish to own some gold. You may choose to purchase coins or bullion. Some of my coins are valuable because of their rarity. These are generally considered of "investment quality." For the most part, however, I have simply purchased gold coins currently being produced by the governments of various countries. I find these the most convenient to purchase and, since I'm not an avid coin collector, find that I don't get embroiled in what I consider the unconscionable markups that many coin dealers insist on receiving for their rare coins. If you would like to purchase some of these "bullion" coins, you may do so from a number of dealers, as well as from some banks or directly from the U.S. government.

In addition to holding physical gold, there is another way in which I believe we can benefit from an uptick in gold prices. Remember, inflation isn't dead—merely sleeping. There will be a time, sooner rather than later, when the Federal Reserve Board, to counteract (or chase) the next recession, will begin furiously pumping dollars into the nation's banking system. When this occurs, you can be certain that gold stocks and gold mutual funds will lead the way out of the recession. I suggest that you familiarize yourself with three possible avenues for participating in the next significant primary move up in gold stocks: closed-end funds that hold gold bullion, closed-end funds that invest in gold-mining stocks, and open-end funds that invest in gold-mining stocks. The individual mining stocks are much more highly leveraged than the price of gold on any given day would indicate. If it costs a company $250 to get the gold out of the ground and gold sells at $250, there is no profit. If bullion sells at $500, anyone holding bullion has doubled his or her money; but the gold-mining company has gone from zero earnings to $250 in earnings for every ounce of gold it mines. Leverage is therefore the big reason to be an investor in gold-mining stocks rather than holding bullion or coins (though, as always, leverage cuts both ways!). The other important consideration is that many gold-mining companies pay a dividend. No dividend is usually paid on physical gold.

Should you decide to buy one of the closed-end funds that holds bullion, you have a number to choose from. When you purchase shares in one of these closed-end funds, you don't get the leverage you would if you were purchasing individual mining shares instead. However, you also don't run the risk of experiencing any of the unpleasant surprises that are based on problems generic to the mining industry but not to the price of bullion.

You may choose instead to purchase shares of closed-end or open-end gold-related mutual funds. These funds invest primarily in gold-mining stocks. You can choose funds that specialize in companies in various parts of the world, such as funds that invest only in U.S., U.S. and Canadian, or U.S., Canadian, and Mexican companies. It's up to you to do your homework and choose the best fund for you.

The one precious metals area I would *not* recommend are the penny gold-mining stocks. While it's true that many of them can have significant price moves, it's also very difficult to get real information regarding their fundamentals. If some broker tells you over the phone that a major discovery is about to be made in the Yukon Territory that will send this company skyrocketing, you have no way of knowing if it's true. Unless you have hired, as one of your coaches, one of the newsletter writers who has a long-term history of success in the precious-metals field, don't even think about the penny mining stocks. Even if you do subscribe to one of these newsletters, take what you read there, even from the most conservative advisor with the finest track record, with a grain of salt.

How will you know when it's time to buy the gold funds? The same way you now know how to determine the bottom of any market: when all the experts tell you that we are in the midst of a grievous and inescapable recession, that inflation is dead, that the real danger now is deflation rather than inflation, and that gold is headed for $35 an ounce. When all the experts are predicting lower prices, start buying.

That wraps it up for the five investment events we need to be sufficiently familiar with to do well in—to place, if not to win. Now let's move on to the other five investment events of our investment decathlon—the ones that we must excel at if we are to win.

CHAPTER 12

WINNING: FIVE EVENTS WE MUST MASTER

Well, competitors, here's what it all comes down to. In the last chapter we discussed five events in which we want to do well in order to keep our overall point totals high. We had to place in those five events. In the five events discussed in this chapter, we must win. These are the five in which we've decided to break the records.

That doesn't mean these are riskier investment choices. By mastering these five events completely, we match our talents with the right events. They aren't riskier, they're just *our* events. We own them. The five events to master are:

1. Buying and selling the common stocks that, today, nobody else wants.
2. Buying, selling, and hedging with convertible bonds and preferreds.
3. Selling short.
4. Buying and selling warrants, SCOREs, "long-term" options, and IPs.
5. Buying, selling, and switching growth and total-return mutual funds and closed-end funds.

BUYING AND SELLING UNPOPULAR COMMON STOCKS

The first event we will master is the art of buying stocks that no one wants today and selling them when everyone wants them tomorrow. You'll recall from our earlier discussion that roughly one-half to five-eighths of the move in any given security can usually be attributed to the move in the market in general, one-quarter to three-eighths of its appreciation is attributable to the industry it's in, and only one-eighth to one-quarter of the price jump is related to the individual security itself. For this reason, many successful investors merely assess whether they are in a primary uptrend or primary downtrend and, rather than buy individual stocks at all, instead invest in growth or total-return mutual funds.

Nonetheless, after you've satisfied yourself that the market is in a primary uptrend (all the indicators you'll want to look at in making this decision are reviewed in the next chapter), you'll be presented with many opportunities to purchase individual common stocks. Should you do so? The answer is a resounding yes. But remember, it makes no sense whatsoever to seek a "moderate" return when making the decision to buy common stocks. Do you look for restaurants that advertise "moderately" good food? Are you satisfied with a "moderately" good sex life? No? Then why *seek* a moderate return in your investing? The marketplace is a great leveler. You'll have plenty of moderate-return situations without *looking* for them. Don't set out in search of them. Set out in search of remarkable value and you will, more often than not, be remarkably well rewarded for your endeavors.

Does this mean that, in an attempt to find very large gains, you should be fully invested at all times? No. Wouldn't you rather have only one position (if that's all you can identify as meeting all your criteria) that turns into one winner than have ten stocks, six of which are losers and four of which are winners? Most people, knowingly or unknowingly, would choose the latter. They would consider *this* a "diversified portfolio." The idea of a diversified portfolio, however, is safety. If you have only one position but the rest of your investing dollars are in T bills or money market funds, you've got the safety that diversification was supposed to supply.

At market tops, virtually all stocks are loved. If you observe the rules in the next chapter regarding the timing of your investments, you will be reluctant to seek out any securities near market tops. Even if you do, you will be virtually unable to find any that meet the criteria you are going to estabish. The positions we seek are often unavailable near market tops because we are not interested in scalping a point or two or three but, rather, in seeking 100 to 1,000 percent moves. When doing so, we are looking for an issue we are so confident of that we feel very comfortable putting a large amount of our total investable funds into that single situation. All too often, I've heard investors say, "Well, what the hell. After all, I'm only buying 200 shares." The question you must always strive to answer is, "If I had the funds, would I buy 2,000 shares?" Or, more appropriately, "Would I sell everything I currently own in order to be involved in this issue?" This discipline does not demand that you do, in fact, sell everything else you own—but you'd better be able to answer this question in the affirmative or there is no sense in entering into it.

As Gerald Loeb observed over a half-century ago:

> The bargains which must be sought to raise investment performance out of the average class, in which net losses occur, into the exclusive class of those who make and keep profits *are not available except occasionally* [emphasis mine]. It should be recognized also that such opportunities will inevitably be available principally when the majority of buyers of securities refuses, because of fear, to take advantage of low prices. Just as inevitably, *the opportunities will not be available when securities are generally popular and eagerly bought* [emphasis again mine]. It should be axiomatic that the successful investor will keep his capital idle in times of popular over-investment and over-confidence.

Okay, so you think you've got enough ice water in your veins to be able to buy securities when they are unpopular, when their industries are out of favor, and when the market in general is scaring the living daylights out of everyone around you. So far, so good. Now let's take a look at where you find these undiscovered gems.

Remember, there are three things that can happen to a stock once you purchase it: It can go up, it can go down, or it can remain the same. It's our job to find stocks that others have sold because they're off chasing the latest penny-stock mining venture or because they're convinced that the stock market is no place for them and are putting all their money into desert land in Arizona. Of all the tens of thousands of securities available for our consideration, there are fewer than 1,000 that institutions regularly follow and place in their investment portfolios. It's pretty tough to find stocks nobody wants in this category. By definition, *somebody* wants it—if all those institutions have discovered it, so have a number of individuals.

The next category consists of all those issues, probably under 1,000 as well, which the institutions are aware of but which very few of them have taken any position in. These are often the types of securities you'll find in the portfolios of the Berkshire Hathaways, the Mutual Shares, the Nicholas Funds, and the Templeton Funds—value investors who, like yourself, are seeking the stocks that no one else wants. You can find tremendous value in these out-of-favor stocks. Usually, these are companies that were well-regarded but have stumbled temporarily. When a few quality institutions like these own shares in the stock you are looking at, that's a good sign. When every single institution in America owns it, it isn't.

Finally, there are all those stocks that are currently too small to be of interest to the institutions or, for whatever reason, have been rejected in the fast by the institutional investors. Many times, these companies were rejected for a very good reason, but that reason is now history. The current reality for the company has radically changed since the institutions abandoned it. Looking for gems like these—stocks that nobody wants to buy today—will often yield some absolute delights, which the institutions will eventually discover or rediscover. Sooner or later, the word gets around about bargains like these. A company cannot forever increase its sales and real earnings and return to its shareholders without investors catching on and, like bulls in a china shop, stampeding to get their piece of the action.

Price-earnings (P/E) ratios are one way to identify these kinds of companies. You'll recall from previous chapters that I retain a healthy skepticism about the various accounting methods that companies can use to inflate or deflate their reported earnings. Nonetheless, taken with a grain of salt (allowing for some variance between real and reported), P/E ratios can still be valuable when used in concert with common sense. The P/E ratio is nothing more than a convenient rule of thumb for evaluating whether a company's stock is priced fairly or not. If a company has "declared" earnings of $1 per share and it currently sells at $15, we say that it has a price-earnings ratio of 15 to 1 or, to simplify, a P/E of 15. While companies can play fast and loose with their accounting in the short term, over the long term it catches up to them. That's why, when we look at P/E ratios over any length of time or over any large number of securities, they become far more valuable than when viewed in isolation at a given point in time. *Generally speaking, those companies which sport lower P/Es are, by definition, the stocks nobody wants to own today.* If two companies each earn (or at least report earning) $1 per share for the trailing 12-month period, and one of them sells at $10 and the other at $20, you can bet that many more people want to own the one selling at $20 or they wouldn't have bid it up to a higher P/E ratio. That's how we'll know that the one selling at $10, or a P/E of 10, is the one (of these two) that nobody wants to own today and is therefore the one that we are more likely to want to own.

Another yardstick we can use is known as the *price-to-sales (P/S) ratio.* The P/S ratio may be Charles Allmon's contribution to intelligent investing, or it may be someone else's, but it's Kenneth L. Fisher who is most closely associated with it. Ken is a money manager, a regular *Forbes* columnist, and the author of the book *Super Stocks,* which I heartily recommend to you. Ken has done for value/fundamental analysis what others have done for technical analysis: updated some of the best thinking from previous generations, added his own thoughts, stirred it all together, and served it up in a way that's very easy on the palate. Ken may not have been the first to utilize P/S ratios, but he's certainly been the driving force in popularizing the concept. P/S ratios have been used by Charles Allmon for a quarter of a century and have certainly been effective for Allmon and his clients. It probably didn't hurt that Ken's father is Philip Fisher, one of the all-time great investment minds in the Western world.

In further developing the concept, I'll let Ken speak for himself in describing the basic idea:

> The price-sales ratio is just like a price-earnings ratio that uses corporate sales instead of corporate earnings. It is the total market value of a company divided by the last 12 months' corporate

sales. To calculate the market value, multiply the stock price by the total number of shares of stock in existence.

Ken's premise is that we should view an investment as if we were a private buyer considering the purchase of the entire business, not just a few or a few hundred or a few thousand shares. The price we'd be willing to pay for this business will be a function of what we expect future sales to be and what profit margin we expect to make on those sales.

What the price-sales ratio really shows is what, at any given time, the market is willing to pay for every dollar of a corporation's sales. Like P/E ratios, P/S ratios measure how popular a company is with investors at a given point in time. We pay a lot for popularity—usually in the form of lost opportunity. To determine a company's P/S ratio, we simply take that company's sales for the trailing 12 months, on a per-share basis, and determine what percentage of that figure the company's common stock is selling for. For instance, in the example we used above for the P/E ratio, if a company has 10 million shares outstanding and $100 million in sales and the stock sells for $10, we say that each share accounts for $10 of its sales and, since it sells at $10 per share, it has a P/S of 1.0. If its sales were $25 million, then, on a per-share basis, we can say that $10 worth of sales are allocable to each share. Since the company sells at $10 this would be a P/S ratio of 4 to 1 or, more simply, a P/S of 4. At this point, even though the P/E seems relatively low (10, as determined above), the P/S yardstick indicates that the company is no bargain. Stocks that sell for P/S ratios of 0.5 to 0.75 are the ideal candidates, when we can find them. Of course, the company, the industry, and the general direction of the market itself determine what a reasonable P/S ratio is for any particular company. For instance, one of the "rules" in *Super Stocks*, for basic-industry manufacturing concerns, is to buy them at a P/S of under 0.4 and sell them whenever they approach 0.8. Yet Ken Fisher's general rule is to seek companies with a P/S of 0.75 or less for purchase candidates—right where he'd recommend selling the smokestack stocks. Obviously, "average" P/S ratios differ, depending on the company, the industry, and the market.

We can't blindly buy low-P/S-ratio stocks in hopes of gain, any more than we can blindly use any other "system." But, as a way of measuring the temporary unpopularity of an issue, it's tough to beat a combination of the P/E ratio and the P/S ratio.

The whole idea of buying stocks that no one else wants to buy today is to buy somewhere around the low area and sell somewhere around the high area. You're not trying to find the exact bottom or the exact top. It's enough, using common sense and the valuation methods we've discussed, to be buying in the general vicinity of the low and selling in the general vicinity of the high. If you buy a little too soon and the stock declines a bit, don't panic. If the reasons you selected it were valid and remain valid, there's no reason to sell. By the same token, if you purchase a short time after it has already begun moving up, you may have lost only the slightest bit of opportunity. Some stocks take a long time to get going; don't sell them just because they've gone up only a couple of points and you're impatient. You're not here to scalp a couple of points; you're here to win convincingly.

What about the high-multiple (high-P/E or high-P/S) stocks? These are often outstanding companies, leaders in their field that are doing a good job. *But they are already recognized by all investors for so doing.* The problem with them is that, because they have such high P/Es and P/Ss, their sales and earnings potential has already been discounted in the price of the stock. They're already moving so smartly ahead that, for the most part, they are low-percentage plays. We're more interested in those stocks and industries which have fallen temporarily from grace during a down market and which reflect that fact by carrying P/E ratios of 7 or 8 and P/S ratios of 0.5 or 0.6. If, in your search, you can't find any such issues, or common sense tells you that the few you do find are not the bargains they seem, you're probably in the vicinity of a market top. If you buy stocks just because everyone around you is bragging about their profits, you'll soon have something to talk about, too—your losses. Remember also that P/E ratios and P/S ratios are always based on the last year's earnings and sales. There are a number of issues, like the chemicals, drugs, autos, and steels, whose profits in any given year can rise and fall tremendously. That's why, as we said earlier, it's terribly important to look at the P/E and P/S trends over time.

In short, don't buy stocks you think are valued around where they should be; buy those you think are selling well below where they should be. There's just no sense in paying 100 cents on the dollar for a company when so many others are available for 50 cents on the dollar. I've bought many times for less than 50 cents on the dollar. One of my best ever was an oil company that had a string of great earnings until two quarters where everything went bad. The company's cash flow was still great, its management was unequaled, and it had all that oil in the ground. I bought and bought some more, and later sold it to all those people who didn't like it at $20 per share but loved it at $50.

Yet another way to find bargains in common stocks, even acknowledging that published corporate information is subject to interpretation, is to do as Fisher and many, many other value buyers recommend: purchase stock as if you were, instead, being offered the opportunity to purchase 100 percent of this company through a business broker. When you look at the entire company as a going proposition, ask yourself whether it's the kind of company you'd want to sink your entire net worth into. If it isn't, why are you impressed with the fact that it's up a couple of points? Don't be so easily impressed—be a knowledgeable *owner*. This is the technique espoused by a number of savvy investors who use primarily fundamental and psychological techniques in selecting stocks. While Ben Graham is probably the best-known of these in this century, people like Philip Fisher and Warren Buffett are two of its smartest proponents today.

Does it work? Well, Warren Buffett's company, Berkshire Hathaway, is a publicly traded company. The company is also a medium for investing in other companies. In 1967 the stock sold for $17 and change; by the end of 1984 it was selling at $1,300 per share. Thanks in part to all of those johnny-come-latelies who have now seen value where only Buffett and a few others saw it in the late 1970s, Berkshire Hathaway in 1987 sold for more than $3,000 per share. Works for him.

Among the "rules" that Buffett outlined in one of his own annual reports to his shareholders is that he looks for *consistent* earnings power (stressing that he doesn't care what analysts predict its earnings *will* be, only what they have been historically), little or no debt, a good return on the common stock equity, and a business that was simple to understand (saying, "I want to be in businesses so good that even a dummy can make money"). He also stressed that *very seldom* is it possible to make a reasonable return by buying companies with high P/E ratios.

There is a final benefit in seeking companies with low stock prices relative to their current sales and earnings power: they're very attractive to other companies. As a result, by consistently seeking such companies, we are often the pleasantly surprised recipients of a tender offer from other companies wishing to purchase the shares from us at significantly higher prices. That is, we often "catch" takeovers and buybacks along with the other insiders—just because our selection criteria are so exacting.

Want to pull away from the pack and win the investment decathlon? Buy the stocks that nobody loves today. When all the rest of the investors decide, months from now, that they want to own shares in those companies, they'll have to buy them from someone. You'll have already crossed the finish line, cooled down, had a refreshing glass of water, and can calmly step up and be the one to sell it to the clamoring crowd.

BUYING AND SELLING CONVERTIBLE SECURITIES

There's nothing like buying a stock that nobody wants to own today—unless it's buying a convertible bond or convertible preferred that nobody wants to own today. Convertible bonds and convertible preferred stocks, you'll recall, pay you a certain specified rate of interest, but also allow you to convert them into a fixed number of shares of the underlying common. The net effect of this is that, in declining markets, you still get a fixed rate of interest on the bond or preferred stock, but in skyrocketing markets you reach a point where you benefit, often dollar for dollar, with the common shareholders.

Convertible bonds are different from convertible preferred stocks. From a strictly legal point of view, the company is obligated to meet its interest payments on the bonds, since they are debt instruments. Since convertible preferred stocks are a form of equity, management can (and sometimes does) reduce or omit dividend payments on them. Of course, before the company can pay any dividends on its common stock, it must make up for all the arrears in the preferred that it was supposed to have paid. In addition, if a company goes bankrupt, the bondholders receive their share of the distribution of the remaining corporate assets before the preferred shareholders do. Preferred shareholders, of course, receive their share of the remaining bits and pieces before any common shareholders do.

Nonetheless, as we've done throughout this book, we'll discuss convertibles as a single item. While there are differences between convertible bonds and convertible preferred stocks, the idea of *any* convertible security is that you can be represented in both the growth and income markets simultaneously. Why would the company give you this right? As you probably recall from our earlier discussions, it's because the company can offer the bond or preferred at a lower yield, thus saving money in interest payments. The same principles apply to seeking good values in convertibles as were discussed above in seeking good values in stocks that nobody wants today. The idea is to find industries and individual companies that are no longer (or not yet) highly regarded by the institutions. If the company's stock has been knocked down, the convertible securities that are tied to it have probably also been knocked down. If interest rates are currently high, the convertible may be cheaper still. It's important always to remember to check whether any company you've decided to take a position in offers a convertible security. You can do so simply by looking at Standard & Poor's stock and bond guides, available at any good public library or directly from Standard & Poor's. Your local broker will also have these guides, but, since convertible securities often carry a lower commission rate (at most firms today, bonds can be purchased for $5 for each $1,000 face-value amount, considerably less than the same broker would make by selling you the common stock), he or she may try to talk you out of it.

How do you evaluate whether a convertible security offers better value than its underlying common stock? The most important thing to look at is its *premium over conversion value* or, more succinctly, its *premium*. What you're seeking by looking at this figure is, basically, how big a move the underlying common has to make before it's worthwhile to convert your convertible security.

Let's take a look at how this works in practice. Let's say we find a stock that we like the looks of: it sells at a P/E of 7 and a P/S of .4, and it's a company we wouldn't mind owning 100 percent of. The only thing is, we're just not certain that the rest of the market will wake up to the value this stock represents. Given this, we might want to see if it has an underlying convertible. Let's say there is, in this case, a convertible bond. The underlying common stock pays no dividend and sells for $30 per share, but the convertible bond pays 7½ percent and is currently priced at $750 per bond. This means that, if you bought ten of these bonds, it would cost you $7,500. You would receive $75 for every $1,000 of *face value* ($10,000 for the ten bonds), so you'd be making about 10% percent in interest income on your investment if it never moved a single point. Let's say that every bond gives you the right to convert into 20 shares of the underlying common stock. Since you have purchased 10 such bonds, this is the equivalent of buying 200 shares of stock, for which you would have had to pay $6,000. The *conversion value* of these bonds is $600. We arrive at this figure as follows: Each bond allows us to buy 20 shares of stock and the current price of the stock is $30 per share, so if we were to convert our bonds today, they would be worth $600 in terms of the underlying common shares. The difference between the $600 and the $750 we paid is known as the conversion premium or premium that we mentioned above.

This premium is the price that we pay for the privilege of having the relative safety of an income-producing asset tied to the good fortunes of the underlying common stock of the company. Of course, in a market decline we would also expect the convertible security to decline less than the underlying common stock. Why is this? Because there are always more income investors out there than there are value investors. As a result, the bond can decline only so much before it becomes, in itself, a much-sought-after commodity purely for the income stream it produces. That is, someone's always willing to buy it for the income it throws off, regardless of whether or not it has a convertible feature. One of the rules of thumb generally used by investors in convertible securities is that they should pay no greater a premium to purchase the convertible bond than they would earn in extra income from the convertible (rather than purchasing the common stock itself) over a three-year period. In our example, the common pays no dividend and the convertible pays about 10 percent a year. That means that, after two years or so, we'll make enough in income from the convertible to pay for the conversion premium of $150. (Remember, we are getting $75 per year in income for each convertible bond we own, versus nothing on the underlying common stock). Finding opportunities like this, we'll probably sleep better and we'll eat every bit as well as if we had purchased the underlying common stock.

Convertible securities represent the best features of both the bond and the stock markets. Savvy investors use them. So should you. In the case of convertible bonds, we need to remember that the bond is considered a loan and you, as the bondholder, are the lender to the company. Unless that company goes bankrupt and has fewer assets available to pay off its debts than it has lenders, the bond is always going to be redeemable at face value upon maturity. Of course, between the time you purchase it and its maturity, it will fluctuate all over the board, just like every other income investment, in reaction to inflation and interest rates. Because of this relative security of capital, income stream, liquidity, and possibility of significant capital gains, I've known a number of individuals with million-dollar-plus portfolios who trade only in convertible securities. Ordinarily, many of these substantial investors shun risk in the marketplace, but with a convertible security, they can actually seek out companies that have wide swings in price. As a matter of fact, the best types of convertibles to invest in are those in which the underlying common stock swings a great deal. There are a number of well-established companies in which the risk of bankruptcy is extremely remote but whose share prices nonetheless fluctuate a great deal.

I view most hedging techniques as generally not worthwhile. I'd rather take the time to do my homework and decide on the direction and probable velocity of the investment I've chosen than continually second-guess myself and try to box myself into a corner by hedging. Nonetheless, there are times when I hedge using convertible bonds. The idea of "hedging" is that we are trying to offset one risk by undertaking another one—that is, using two securities whose prices move in the same direction but at different rates. For instance, we might purchase a convertible bond that is selling very close to its conversion value and sell short shares of its underlying common stock. If we were simply to sell short the common stock, it could rise 100 or 1,000 or 10,000 percent and wipe us out. But if instead we establish a hedged position by buying the convertible bond and selling short the number of common shares into which that bond is convertible, we are in a position to make a good profit. If the price of the common stock falls, the price of the bond will decline less because of all those income investors who will still want to buy the convertible bond purely for its income value. If the price of the common stock surprises us and skyrockets, as long as we purchased the convertible somewhere very near conversion value, the bond price will rise, dollar for dollar, from the conversion-value *parity* point on, in concert with the underlying common stock. ("Parity" refers to the point at which there is no premium over conversion value.) In this case, the gain in the convertible bond offsets the loss in the short position and there is no net loss.

There are all manner of variations on this basic theme, but this is the type of hedging that, alone among all the alternatives, I would recommend. I've used convertible bonds in this manner when I've felt that the market, the industry, and the individual issue were all significantly overpriced and ready to take a tumble. In those cases where I was right, my short-sale profit always more than compensated for any decline in the value of the convertible bond. In those cases where I was wrong and the underlying common continued to appreciate, I was always very relieved that I had hedged my position. Does this eat into your total return? Yes, but, by taking a look at what other nonconvertible bonds are currently yielding, you can get a pretty good sense of how far the convertible will fall in the event that the stock declines. As a result, you can assess the expected percentage return by deducting the relatively predictable loss on the convertible and contrasting it with your profits if the stock is at various prices. Selling short is one of the few cases where I recommend using a hedge, and then I recommend using convertible bonds rather than options or warrants.

SELLING SHORT

Selling short is a key to success in the investment decathlon. Yet most people won't sell short. Something like nine out of 10 individual investors have never even tried to sell short. Talk about your basic golden opportunity! Any time 90 percent of your fellow competitors are unwilling to leave the illusory safety of the pack, you have an opportunity to break away and break the tape.

The first thing you have to do is erase the notion that there is something inherently dangerous *or* unethical about selling short. Specialists and market makers do it all day long and all in the name of maintaining orderly markets. Now, orderly markets are something we all can agree is desirable, so, if short selling is done to stabilize the market, it can't be all bad, right?

When you want to buy a stock and the specialist doesn't have any to sell you, he sells short in order to be able to make good on his obligation to you. Unethical? It's done every day. Remember, for every buyer there's a seller—though they don't always line up in the right order. As in the example of our friend who sold the tickets to the rock concert earlier in the book, sometimes the product is there first, sometimes the demand is there first.

As for the supposed danger in selling short, there's no more danger in selling short than there is in many other investment techniques and only slightly more risk than simply buying a stock (creating a long position). As a matter of fact, selling short into a raging bear market may be the only rational decision and may in fact be safer in that environment than trying to find the one lone stock to buy that goes against the trend and actually goes up. That's not to say there is *no* risk in short selling. There are times when your brokerage firm has a problem delivering to another customer and forces you to cover your position at a time you'd rather not cover. This doesn't happen often, especially with large, actively traded issues but it does represent a potential risk.

You remember that *selling short* involves nothing more than entering a sell order for a security you don't (yet) own. You're betting that the price of the stock will drop and you will buy back the shares you sold. Assuming you buy back at a lower price, you've made a profit. If you sell short 300 shares of Amalgamated Couch Potato Junk Food, Inc., at $30 per share, all you have to do is borrow the shares from your brokerage firm in order to be able to deliver them to the person who bought them. If the stock drops to $15 and you buy it back at this price, you just made $15 × 300 shares, or $4,500.

Short selling is the single most important event to master in a clearly defined bear market. Given that the markets go up about two-thirds of the time and go down one-third of the time, it would be stupid not to take advantage of the biggest opportunity available during that third of the time that the market's heading lower. Not only that, but, since declines typically happen faster than advances, you can often make a great deal of money very quickly by selling short in the right market environment. Let's talk about how to do this right.

As always, there are three factors to consider in selecting a short sale: the market, the industry, and the individual company. And, just as when we select a long position (buy a stock), the market direction itself primarily accounts for whether or not any individual issue will work out, so it is in short selling. If the market is in a free fall, even the good stocks will be carried down with it. If the market is plummeting and the industry our short-sale candidate is in is also weak, so much the better. And, finally, if the stock itself is a dog, we're really on to something.

So what do we look for when seeking the perfect short sale? Exactly the opposite of what we sought when going long. We're looking for a bear market for stocks in general, an industry that's doing very poorly (all other stocks within this group are falling out of bed), and an individual issue that has had a substantial runup in price, then had a wide plateau where, no matter what happened, it just couldn't trade beyond a narrow range and is now heading south.

To illustrate this last part about the individual issue, the best short sale is one in which the stock shot up as a result of hope, hyperbole, or just plain hype. This usually means a meteoric rise with lots of people buying just to get in on the action. Then, the stock should run into trouble and not be able to trade beyond a certain range. This part is important, too, because it means that lots of investors are becoming disillusioned with the stock but lots more who have no profit in it are buying. Thus, when it begins its decline, there are lots of potential sellers who will stick around for the first few points on the down side, thinking it will turn around, then will all panic out at about the same time, putting further downward pressure on the stock.

Very often, these stocks pick up bargain hunters along the way who conclude, usually wrongly, that this erstwhile high-flyer just "has" to turn around. As a result, there are always new groups to be disillusioned and, as a result, the stocks often plunge well below the point where anyone thought they would finally come to rest.

I'll give two examples of this from my own investing. Both companies are still around, though both are losing money faster than an armored truck with its back door open, so I'll be kind and not divulge their names. After all, they were both very good to me.

The first company was an oil exploration and refining company that sold for $12 when I shorted it. The market was weak (in what proved to be a pause in an ongoing bull market), the oil stocks were getting slaughtered, and this company had run up based on some nonsensical buyout story. Looking at the fundamentals, no one in his or her right mind would have bought this company as an ongoing business. Its earnings were way overstated, its P/S ratio was about 6.0, and its management was entrenched, stubborn, and myopic. I thought it might go to $4 to $6 in nine months to a year. In fact, the buyout nonsense evaporated, the real earnings became known, and the stock went to $2 and change, where I covered (bought back the shares). And oh, yes, it did all this in three months and five days.

The second stock was a short seller's dream. It was an also-ran company with negligible earnings (the P/E ratio was over 200) and a terrible P/S, and it was in the wrong industry at the wrong time—it was a fast-food hamburger chain with a dozen outlets and a "concept." A "concept" stock is one that has a supposedly revolutionary process, product, or approach and the term is often a euphemism in brokerese for "This turkey has no earnings, no patents, no management, but, hey, it's got a helluva story." Now, I want you to do me a favor. The next time a stockbroker calls you and tells you that he or she has a "concept" stock, I want you to hang up on them in mid-sentence. More people have made a small fortune—out of a large one—in concept stocks than in almost any other kind of venture.

To make a long story short (no pun—honest), I gave this place one more shot before shorting it. I ate there. You can believe me when I say that no one who ever ate one of this place's cardboardburgers would ever go back or would ever recommend it to anyone he or she cared about. I shorted what we'll call Conceptburger, Inc., touted by many as "the next McDonald's," at $14 and covered it at $2⅞. What's for dessert?

There are a number of investment newsletters that purport to advise investors and help them locate good short-sale candidates. As this is an area of particular interest to me, I think I've tried them all. By and large, I've found them all wanting—except one. I recently discovered a publication called *Overpriced Stock Service (OSS)*. Edited by Michael Murphy, who also produces the *California Technology Stock Letter,* he writes under the apt nom de plume of "Ursae Majoris."

I must say, I have found his candor and style a breath of fresh air in this highly specialized subgenre of investment newsletters. Basically fundamentalist in his approach, Mr. Murphy originally published *OSS* for institutions, but not too long ago he began offering it to individual investors as well. You'll find that he has a good basic approach to the economic environment and a solid grounding in many of the ideas we've discussed in this book: price-to-sales ratios and price-to-earnings ratios, to name just two. The twist, of course, is that Ursae Majoris is looking for precisely the type of stock we're not interested in buying as a long position: those with very high P/S and P/E ratios, lots of insiders selling, and those rated poorly by services that screen stocks as possible purchase candidates.

If there is a drawback to *OSS,* it's that it is an expensive service—maybe too expensive for most individual investors. But if you're an active trader, it's certainly worth looking into.

There is one important caveat to give you before we leave the area of short selling: always, and I mean *always,* place a buy-stop above your short sale. A *buy-stop* is an order that you place with your stockbroker which executes only if the stock rises to the level of the price you indicate. For instance, in the preceding example, when I shorted the stock at $14, I placed a buy-stop order at $17⅛. That way, had the stock risen even though I thought it would fall, my loss would have been limited. When the stock traded at my price, my order would have been activated as a market order. As the stock disintegrated, I placed lower and lower buy-stop orders in order to lock in my profit and protect myself against any sudden price rise. There are no stop orders over the counter, which means that you must actively watch the position and be prepared to exit if it violates a mental buy-stop you've placed at a certain price. If you don't have the discipline to do this, stay away from OTC short sales.

BUYING AND SELLING WARRANTS, SCOREs, "LONG-TERM" OPTIONS, AND IPs

The fourth investing event that we must master in our decathlon is the buying and selling of warrants, SCOREs and long-term options. Let's look first at the Wonderful World of Warrants. You'll recall that *warrants* are basically long-term options to buy stock. They're different from puts and calls in that puts and calls are very short term in nature and in that warrants are issued by the corporations to give the warrant holder the right to purchase that company's securities. Warrants, properly purchased, can give us the same volatility without many of the risks associated with options. Like options, warrants are "wasting assets." The life of most warrants, while fixed, is much longer than for an option. Whereas options are usually issued for three, six, or nine months, warrants are issued for five to 10 or more years. (With some exceptions: there are at least three closed-end mutual funds I know of that have issued perpetual warrants, which are designed to be outstanding for as long as the company exists.) As with options, however, leverage is still the big attraction in warrants. It's not at all uncommon for warrants to appreciate five or 10 times as much as the underlying common stock in an up market.

Let's take the case of a stock selling for $12 that has warrants giving the holder the right to purchase shares at $16. For illustration purposes, let's assume that the warrants have 10 years remaining until expiration. At or near major market bottoms, it wouldn't be at all unlikely for the warrant to have a market price of $1 or so. If the market improves and the underlying common stock takes off, the warrant has no intrinsic value even though the stock goes up to $13, $14, or $15. It will appreciate in price, however, as investors continue to believe that the market move is for real. It's when the underlying common stock is a volatile one that we see the true leverage potential of warrants. If this stock goes to $24, it has doubled from $12. At $24, however, the warrant now has an intrinsic value of $8 (the difference between the $16 at which each warrant may be converted into a share of common stock and its current market price), but it will also have some remaining time value; for our purposes, let's just add a buck, although that's probably quite conservative. This means that the warrant now has a value of $9. So here we have a case where, if the common stock goes from $12 to $24, or goes up by 200 percent, the underlying warrant would likely go from $1 to $9, or 900 percent—nine times our original investment. The biggest leverage in warrants is virtually always found in situations just like this one, where the warrant has no intrinsic value because the stock trades at or below the price at which the warrant may be converted into the stock. Once the warrants begin to develop real intrinsic value, because of the appreciation in price of the underlying common stock, the leverage evaporates rapidly. Of course, if you're the one who was smart enough to buy it at $1, what do you care about the troubles of some johnny-come-lately trying to find a good warrant value six months or a year down the road?

Obviously, in seeking opportunities in warrants, we are looking for underlying securities that have demonstrated a history of rapid price movements. This can readily be found in a number of cyclical stocks. As a general rule, I don't like to buy warrants with less than four or five years of life remaining. Every stock needs time to realize its potential, and much less than four or five years doesn't allow for the occasional surprise. That's precisely why most put and call options aren't worthwhile investments. I would still look at an outstanding warrant opportunity with three years remaining but get increasingly nervous much below this point.

Many investors are rediscovering warrants because of the "currency exchange warrants" issued by many multinational firms like Citicorp, Ford Motor Credit Corp., General Electric Credit Corp., and the Student Loan Marketing Association, a quasi-governmental agency. These warrants allow individual investors to participate in currency fluctuations between major world currencies, offering leverage and low entry cost.

Some warrants have a couple of problems, which we must be aware of. Some of them are "callable"—that is, they may be called in by the company in exchange for some payment to the warrant holder. Since the warrants don't cost the company a thing, I have no earthly idea why it would call them in. But I will say that I don't want to touch such warrants. You can check whether a warrant you're considering has this ridiculous feature (most don't) by checking a number of published sources. One investment newsletter that does a sterling job of discussing warrants is the *RHM Survey of Warrants, Options, and Low-Priced Stocks*. At such time as I believe warrants are close to presenting the kind of opportunity they always do at major bear-market bottoms, I'll hire the folks at RHM by subscribing to their publication. (Incidentally, this firm also covers SCOREs and PRIMEs in this same publication and publishes a sister publication covering convertible bonds.)

The other major problem with some warrants is that, if the company dilutes the value of its stock without recompensing or protecting the warrant holder, the value of your warrant could be diluted. For example, if a company were to announce a three-for-one stock split, each individual share of stock would be worth one-third as much as it had been. For common shareholders, this is no problem. They may have something worth only a third as

much as it was before, but they have three times as much of it. If
the warrant holders aren't protected, however, they could see
their entire investment vanish. Again, there are various publications which assist in avoiding these pitfalls, the *RHM Survey* being the very best, in my opinion.

The only other real risk we run in dealing with warrants is
failing to apply the precepts we've talked about elsewhere in
this book and will take up again in the next chapter. You want
to buy stocks at a reasonable price—that is, you want to buy
them when they are out of vogue. When this happens, their
warrants will offer maximum leverage to match the maximum
volatility of the underlying common stock. This is a risk well
within your ability to control. It's up to you to do your homework
and determine, just as with convertible bonds, whether or not a
stock you are considering purchasing has warrants available as
well.

There are a couple other ways to play the game using
warrants. One is to short expiring warrants and the other is to
hedge using warrants.

Occasionally, a great opportunity will present itself in the
area of shorting an expiring warrant. If your study of the primary indicators (which we'll review in the next chapter) con-
vinces you that we are approaching or are at or have just com-
pleted a major market top, that is a good time to look for warrants that have a short remaining life and that are warrants to
buy exceedingly volatile stocks which have had a strong runup.
The idea here is to find a stock that we expect will fall out of bed
and warrants to purchase shares of this stock that, as the stock
falls, will sink below the level at which they have any intrinsic
value. Let's look at an example. XYZ stock is selling for $18 per
share and has warrants that expire in 18 months and that give
the holder the right to purchase the common stock at $11 per
share. By definition, the warrant must be worth at least $7 (its
intrinsic value) plus any time value. Since we're presuming
we're around a major top, everybody loves stocks and wants to
own them, so we'll add $2 for the time value. If you are con-
vinced that the underlying stock will plummet in the coming
decline and you figure that, a year from now, it will be selling
below $11 and will still be below $11 in a year and six months,

when the warrants expire, you can make out like a bandit. If you shorted the stock and it went to $10, you'd have an $800 profit for every 100 shares shorted. Tie up $1,800 ($900 if buying on margin), make $800. Not bad. But if you shorted the warrant, you'd have tied up $900 ($450 on margin) and made $900. The only thing more fun than selling something at $9 and covering it at zero is having it given to you at zero and watching it go to $9.

Are there any pitfalls to this strategy? Of course there are! Primarily two: the stock could continue rising and we'd have a loss on the warrant position, or the issuing company could extend the life of the warrant, in which case it wouldn't expire and we'd have to risk its eventual rise again in the next bull market. Shorting expiring warrants is a riskier analog to our primary investing event, buying warrants. While not a primary event, it is a way to make money, especially in a bear market.

Hedging with warrants is also a riskier side event. Given that warrants are more volatile than the common, they can be used to hedge a position. As we said earlier, a hedge is created when two securities travel in the same direction but at different velocities. To hedge the position described above, for instance, we might short the expiring warrant but buy the underlying common. If the stock keeps going up, the warrant and stock would counteract each other for no gain and no loss (or, more accurately, for a gain that exactly equaled the amount of the loss). If the stock declines, the warrant can be expected to fall faster, resulting in a smaller (hedged) profit. Get some experience and read up in greater depth before playing with these.

We've talked previously about PRIMEs and SCOREs. PRIMEs, you recall, tend to be purchased by individuals interested in safety and income. They give the holder the right to all dividends declared by the underlying common stock and a small amount of the appreciation potential. SCOREs function pretty much the same way that warrants do, with one difference. SCOREs are issued against (currently) 26 of the bluest of the blue chips. These are those institutional favorites which will inevitably fall from grace during the major market declines and, while their securities languish in the next bear market, the companies themselves will be tightening up and making plans to bust out during the next market and economic expansion. At such time as these blue chips are battered so mercilessly that no one likes them, I'll be jumping in with both feet and buying SCOREs on them. Assuming that there are three or more years remaining, I expect to be able to buy the equivalent of a three-year warrant on the best of the best for just a few dollars each. It's a little difficult to get information on these undiscovered gems right now, although the *RHM Survey* as well as *Professional Investor* and some other savvy investment advisory services have begun to look at them. About halfway or two-thirds of the way through the *next* bull market, everyone will realize that SCOREs were a great opportunity for appreciation and will be touting them left and right. Having read this far, it goes without saying that you'll be one of the few clever players who'll be more than happy to sell to all those clamoring to buy the SCOREs that you purchased so much more cheaply.

There are two relatively new areas we need to review: long-term options and Index Participation Contracts (IPs). The American Stock Exchange pioneered long-term options and has recently developed options for one, two, and three years on its Institutional Index. The Institutional Index is an index of institutional favorites—stocks widely held by the greatest number of institutions. The Institutional Index has traditionally had one-, two-, and three-, as well as six- and nine-month, options available. By adding the one-, two-, and three-year expiration dates, options on this index have become far more attractive. Premiums may sometimes be out of line because, during periods of extreme market volatility, nobody's sure which way the market's going to jump and option writers are still expecting a very high premium. Of course, they are assisted in this endeavor by the large number of purchasers who are willing to pay these high premiums in anticipation of a truly major move. Since the American Exchange has made the decision to continue to open up new three-year option series on a rolling basis, we know that we can always get a long-term call or put with three years left to run. As the premiums contract to a more reasonable level, many investors look very closely at this "pseudo-warrant" as a way to benefit from the foibles of those who buy at the top and sell at the bottom and their not-much-better-off brethren, those who hold on through thick and thin.

IPs, on the other hand, are more like common stocks than they are like options. Like warrants, SCOREs, and long-term options, they are "derivative investments." You'll recall that they pay dividends quarterly, have no expiration date, and are based on an index of underlying securities. IPs offer the independent investor the opportunity to play "the market" rather than individual issues, because they track the general market indexes. IPs are a much better deal for investors than index options—and couldn't have been introduced at a time when individuals were more in need of a better deal!

BUYING, SELLING, AND SWITCHING GROWTH AND TOTAL-RETURN MUTUAL FUNDS

The final event that we must master to ensure maximum success in our investing decathlon is the buying, selling, and switching of growth and total-return open- and closed-end mutual funds. We have already said a great deal about the uses of mutual funds. I myself have hired a number of mutual fund managers to assist me in reaching my goals by purchasing shares of their funds. Now, since I'm in the investing business and have immediate access to all the latest technological gadgets and more tips and rumors than I want to hear, and since I am generally disdainful of the institutions *as a group* in their ability to outperform either the market or me, why would I hold money in these funds? The answer is that, as in all other endeavors of living, there are a few brave, bright, and contrary souls who prove the rule by being the exception. To these gifted individuals, my hat goes off. As a matter of fact, my hat is off and my wallet is out. I keep a certain number of dollars safely away from any proclivity I might have to overtrade by placing them with a few good mutual fund managers.

Make no mistake: many mutual funds have an abysmal record at managing money. In any given market, up or down, roughly half the mutual funds will outperform the Dow by some incremental amount, and roughly half will underperform it by some incremental amount. We can get results like that by throwing darts at a board. Nonetheless, there are a few who, over time, have demonstrated the ability to make money for their investors year in and year out, market up or market down. That's not to say that they will necessarily make money during market declines. During any decline you must make the decision whether or not it's worth it to you to remove your money from the mutual fund, either by taking it out or by switching it to one of their money market funds.

Fidelity is probably the biggest family of mutual funds. At last count, Fidelity had 25 or so income funds, 30 or so growth and total-return funds, 35 or 40 sector funds, and various money market and tax-free money market funds. Yet even this mighty leviathan has its difficulties beating the market. Only one out of four of its growth funds in operation for longer than five years had done better than the Dow Jones Industrial Averages for the period 1982 to 1987. Only one of three funds in operation for 10 years had done so. In both these cases it was the same fund, their Magellan Fund. Of course, if you had been lucky enough to be invested in this particular fund, you would have seen a 177 percent increase for the five-year period and an incredible increase of almost 1,500 percent for the 10-year period. (Now *that's* professional full-time management.) Are many investors willing to pay for that kind of performance? Of course! They're willing to pay by paying the mutual funds' expenses and their loads as well. You recall from Chapter 3 that I won't tell you that no-load funds are the only way to go. I will say that, if a no-load fund can give you the same return as a load fund, you're obviously better off purchasing the no-load and saving the 3 to 9 percent commission fee. I can also say that, *as a group,* no-load funds perform as well as or better than load funds. But since you're not buying the entire group of no-load funds or the entire group of load funds, you must select a fund on the basis of its historical track record, performance in bull markets and bear markets, the philosophy of the people running it, how that philosophy coincides with or contradicts your own, and whether, upon studying its prospectus, you would feel comfortable owning the portfolio of securities in which it is currently invested.

So how do I go about selecting these special few funds in which to place significant amounts of my net worth? Well, we pilots have a saying: "There are old pilots and there are bold pilots, but there are no old, bold pilots." What this means, in the investing arena, is that time winnows out the witless, the idiots, the wet-behind-their-ears MBAs, the one-trick ponies, and the just plain lucky managers who happened to catch the last bull market with a collection of overly volatile securities. Information is available from a number of publications, including *Money Magazine, Changing Times,* and *Consumer Reports,* but for my money the *Forbes* Honor Roll is the best single source of information regarding mutual funds which have done well in good markets and bad over a long period of time. I like to be invested in funds where the managers have white hair, not white knuckles. I want their white-knuckle days to be behind them, and I want them to be sharp enough to have survived intact. Many investors choose to invest on the basis of the fund manager, like buying Fidelity's Magellan Fund because Peter Lynch is the fund manager. He may not have white hair, but he's definitely earned his stripes. Mutual Shares, run by Michael Price, remains a favorite of many through good markets and bad. These gentlemen and their staff spend long hours reviewing special situations that you or I would have to hire a whole team to duplicate. But why should we? If we hire them, we get the same benefit without any labor problems and without having to pay employees' social security taxes. Other investors might choose the Nicholas Fund, where Albert Nicholas seeks out those same low-P/E stocks we discussed earlier in this chapter. Then there's Templeton Growth, a bit more volatile and less dependable in bear markets perhaps than these others, but then, that's the price you pay to have the venerable John Templeton on your team. The nice thing about having pros like this on your own personal investing payroll is that, even after they've decided to take life a little easier, they've usually made certain that they have found like-minded individuals to carry on the work they've begun. Another frequently selected fund is the closed-end fund, Growth Stock Outlook, headed by Charles Allmon.

One thing to bear in mind about all these funds: we don't buy a mutual fund or a portfolio of companies, we hire *people.* In virtually all these cases, the people at the top have been there for a very, very long time. Should this change—either these people are no longer there or they no longer follow the precepts that have made them so successful as investors—we might want to consider leaving them and hiring some new managers whom we think will do a better job. You will note one other thing about the above funds. There are load funds, low-load funds, no-load funds, and closed-end funds. If we can make 1,500 percent in Fidelity Magellan, we should feel a little silly about balking at a 3 percent load. If John Templeton can turn $10,000 into $800,000 in 31 years, we should feel positively stupid about balking at paying 8½% up front.

During the next major market decline, many investors will be reviewing the closed-end funds much more thoroughly. Remember, closed-end mutual funds, with their fixed amount of capital already secure, can be much more flexible in down markets. Unlike the open-end mutual funds, they're not confronted with a sudden influx of capital from uninformed investors right at the market's top, which would virtually *force* them to be fully invested near market tops in order to keep their shareholders happy. Nor do they have the problem of having thousands of disgruntled investors redeeming their funds at the absolute bottom, leaving them with no money to participate in the marketplace just when they should be most active. This combination of factors is what makes it so difficult for most mutual funds to outperform the market averages. Also, a number of very savvy and value-oriented players, including the aforementioned Charles Allmon, Martin Zweig, Charles Royce, and Mario Gabelli, have established closed-end funds in recent years.

One other comment regarding mutual funds: this is about the only investment vehicle in which I believe in dollar-cost averaging. As previously discussed, I think dollar-cost averaging is a bill of goods sold to an unsuspecting public as regards individual issues of common stock. There is a very dangerous presumption in dollar-cost averaging that depressed stocks always recover. They don't. Depressed mutual funds, however, usually do. That's why, while I normally sell most securities prior to bear markets, in some cases I've not tried to second-guess the marketplace with all my dollars, but have kept some money in certain mutual funds and have no problem dollar-cost averaging by simply buying more shares of these funds at lower prices. In other cases I've used the "telephone switch privileges" that many funds provide and, with a single phone call, have removed my funds from the marketplace and put them instead into a money market fund run by the same mutual fund company. All other things being equal, I'll always choose a fund group with such switch privileges over one that doesn't have them.

If you master the five investment events outlined in this chapter and become good enough to use, where appropriate, the five events discussed in the preceding chapter, you are virtually guaranteed success in the marketplace. All that remains is to make certain that you time your purchases and sales appropriately. That's the subject of the next chapter, in which we'll review and summarize the various "tricks of the trade" that will allow you to discern when we are at major market bottoms or major market tops.

CHAPTER 13

KNOWING WHEN TO MAKE YOUR MOVE

Timing Is Everything

Just as all athletes have to time their moves in order to pull away from the pack at exactly the right moment, so must you be able to time your moves in order to distance yourself from the great bulk of investors who will be tripping all over themselves and trampling one another at all major market turning points. The basics we will review here will allow you to determine the broad trends of the marketplace. The basic lesson that we must learn is: don't fight the tape! All the investing events described in Chapters 11 and 12 will serve you well in up markets. In down markets, you'll need to find some good contrary ideas. Perhaps you'll want to short the overpriced favorites, using underlying convertible bonds to hedge your risk. Perhaps you'll find investments that are in their own private bull market even while most common stocks are in a bear market; this occasionally happens with bonds, gold stocks, or investments tied to the U.S. or other currencies. The point is that you want to determine *primary market trends,* not the day-to-day, week-to-week, or even month-to-month blips that will do nothing more than confuse you if you try to play every one of them.

This may be the single most difficult lesson to learn. Most investors lose sight of the simple truths presented in this book when confronted with the bewildering array of conflicting opinion, advice, and short-term market action. By doing nothing more than playing the primary trends intelligently, you can make more money than you've ever dreamed possible. Why screw it up by trying to trade every 50 or 100 or 150 points up or down in the Dow?

Short-term forecasting is brutally difficult, if not impossible. Flight-center meteorologists can tell the pilots where the thunderstorms are, but not the individual wind shears. It's much easier to predict the tides than it is the individual waves. The same is true in investing. If you are smart enough to have come this far, don't throw it all away now. In this chapter we'll talk about determining how to read the primary market trends and knowing when to buy and when to sell *individual* securities.

In his superb book, *Stock Market Logic: A Sophisticated Approach to Profits on Wall Street,* Norman G. Fosback points out the importance of timing the primary market trends. He looked at the period from early 1964 through the end of 1975 and noted that the average common stock on the New York Stock Exchange provided a total return from dividends and capital appreciation of 55 percent. Given his time frame, that's less than a 4 percent compounded return per year and, as he pointed out, was actually, after inflation was taken into account, a negative return. By comparison, an investor who did nothing more than remove his or her funds from the marketplace during the three bear markets that occurred over this time, his or her return would have been almost *800 percent,* or *20 percent* per annum compounded. This return was not a matter of superior stock selection, but merely of buying and selling "the market," as if by using an index mutual fund. Fosback then took his study one step further and looked at what would have happened if an investor had also sold this same market index short during those three bear markets. In this case, our mythical investor would have gained an additional 11 percent per year profit during this period for a total annual return, compounded, of 31 percent, or *2,368 percent* versus the 55 percent that a buy and hold strategy would have provided. Now you know why I'm not so hot on the buy and hold approach. Of course, given the advent of money market funds and higher interest rates in recent years, alternatives now exist to short selling wherein we could have done almost as well by simply removing our funds from the market and placing them in a money market fund.

This simple illustration should serve to point out how absolutely critical timing is in winning the investment decathlon. All too many people think, quite incorrectly, that they always have to keep their money "working" for them. Of course, this presumes that their money will really be working for them and not against them. That's an incorrect assumption. At the point of risk, it isn't your money. It's just money. Whether it comes back to you multiplied many times over or finds its way into someone else's pockets depends, in great part, on your ability to shed this notion that your money always has to be working. There are many times when it's best to take a break. Pull yourself out of the market and take a fresh look at things. You'll do far better in the long run. Those people who tell you you must always keep your money working are probably the same people who go to work sick rather than take a day off to get better. Sure, they didn't waste a day—they wasted a week because, by overdoing it, they got sicker. The same is true in the market; you can lose a day—or a dollar—here and there, but that's a lot better than losing a week—or your entire portfolio—later.

Being willing to leave the market from time to time, without having your money on the line, allows you to be more levelheaded in assessing the current condition of the marketplace. Remember, popular sentiment should be bearish and stocks in general not at all well-regarded at the time you choose to commit serious money to the market. The individual issues you choose and the industries you select should be perceived by the public at large as pretty dumb places to put money at this time. There are points in any market cycle where even the best securities become unloved, and that's when opportunity knocks loudest. It doesn't happen often, but when it does, you want to be ready for it. By buying consistently when everyone else thinks putting money in the market is a ridiculous thing to do and by selling when everyone else thinks the market is the only place to put their money, we're always assured that we can buy at the right price and sell to others at the right price. The way we do this is by discerning the general trend and buying securities when most of them are selling for eight or 10 times earnings and selling them when most of them are selling for 20 or 30 times earnings. You figure it out: why is it that people won't touch a stock when it's selling at eight times earnings, but, two years later at the top of the next bull market, when it's selling at 30 times earnings, they think it's the best thing ever?

Having made the decision to act decisively and in concert

with the primary trends, how do you determine when you are in a primary bull market or a primary bear market? We've talked about some of the indicators already, but we'll review them here. Listed below are the five that I use without fail as well as ten others that I find helpful.

THE FIVE PRIMARY MARKET-TIMING TOOLS

1. The dividend yield of the Dow Jones Industrial Averages. Whenever the dividend yield on the Dow Averages approaches 3 percent, I believe that the market has attracted entirely too much interest from individuals and institutions. If they have bid prices up so high that the dividend yield on these classic blue-chip stocks is in the 3 percent area, I am concerned that, maybe not today and maybe not tomorrow but somewhere right around in here, we're in the topping area that leads to sharp, nasty market breakdowns.

Conversely, when the dividend yield on the Dow Jones Industrials approaches 6 percent or higher, money usually starts flowing into the market. There are two reasons for this. The first is that common stocks paying a 6 percent or greater dividend yield usually look pretty attractive to income purchasers who see a viable alternative to bonds in the Dow Jones Industrials; they can get 6 or 7 percent interest here *and* get an equity kicker. The second reason this zone looks very good to me is that it means that most investors haven't been attracted to the market even though they can get a 6 percent or greater yield. If the investing public feels that there's no reason to be in the marketplace, it's time for me to jump in.

2. The book value of the Dow Jones Industrial Averages. *Book value* is a reflection of what a company would be worth if it were liquidated tomorrow and its assets sold to other companies at fair market value. Whenever the Dow Jones Industrials, as a group, approach two times book value or more, again I start getting a little nervous. This is roughly the time to be selling. By the same token, when the Dow Jones Industrials' book value is such that all these stocks put together sell at 1 to 1.2 times book value, it's definitely time for me to look at them.

3. When I see the P/E ratio on the Dow Jones Industrial Average down in the 10 to 12 range, as far as I'm concerned it's time to begin quietly buying. When the Dow Industrials have a P/E ratio of 18 to 20 or more, it's time to leave the party.

4. When the Federal Reserve Board, by selling securities, raising the reserve requirement, or raising the discount rate, indicates that it is tightening the screws on the money supply, it's time for me to bid a fond adieu to the marketplace. Conversely, when the Fed is pumping money into the system by buying securities, lowering the reserve requirement at banks, or lowering its discount rate, I figure it's trying to tell me something. All I have to do is listen.

5. If rock-solid market commentators who represent mainstream, establishment money-management firms, banks, and pension funds are all quoted in the financial press as despairing of ever seeing an uptick again, it's time for me to step in and buy. By the same token, when they start telling me I'm in that proverbial new era of investing where the old rules no longer apply, I've got news for them: the old rules still do apply, and one of those rules is that I should get out of the marketplace.

These are the five primary indicators that tell me, with remarkable clarity, brevity, and accuracy, what kind of market I'm in. All are readily available for my perusal. The first three are all listed together every single day under the "Psychological Indicators" section of the "General Market Indicators" page in *Investor's Daily* or weekly in *Barron's.* The fourth is available in *Barron's, Investor's Daily* and *The Wall Street Journal,* and the fifth in every paper and on every TV in America. If they don't suggest we're at a primary turning point, then I presume that the trend I'm already experiencing is unbroken and until I see all the evidence of one of these primary turning points, I continue with the kinds of actions I have most recently been taking. If that action has been to buy stocks, convertibles, warrants, SCOREs, precious metals, or mutual funds, then I continue to hold them, *no matter what the short-term ups and downs of the marketplace,* until I see evidence of a major turning point. If my most recent action has been to sell, then I don't jump back in just because some presidential spokesman says everything is going to be hunky-dory. I wait for the above five signs of the primary turn.

10 ADDITIONAL MARKET-TIMING TOOLS

At any given time, remember, one or two indicators may not be in sync with the others. So here are ten others, which I use primarily when the above five indicators are giving me mixed signals.

1. When you see hundreds of new lows being made by various securities day after day, you're probably in the general vicinity of a primary bottom. When you see hundreds of new highs being recorded day after day, welcome to the virtual end of the bull market.

2. When cartoonists start poking fun at the tough times on Wall Street, it's probably time to reenter the market. I'm indebted to Yale Hirsch and his *Stock Trader's Almanac* for this delightful piece of contrarian thinking. Hirsch puts out his *Almanac* yearly, and it's chock full of wonderful tidbits, quotes, and wisdom about the stock market. Hirsch's speculation as to why this "cartoonist indicator" is successful is that cartoonists, like most of the population who don't actively follow the market, aren't normally aware of events occurring on Wall Street. However, a major debacle (or sense of euphoria) will get their attention. Since it's massacres that make for good cartoons, these cartoonists are much better at showing market bottoms than market tops. The idea is that, as the market itself becomes front-page news, cartoonists just naturally, in the course of looking for ideas, find themselves thinking about the market. As soon as cartoonists start making fun of investors, brokers, or Wall Street in general, it's probably a pretty good time to buy.

3. When the magazines and newspapers that make up the financial press announce record revenues and get thicker and thicker, look out below! Record revenues in financial publications come not from subscriptions, although those go up in up markets as well, but from advertising revenue. When all the promoters have money to spend on advertising, it's because investors have been giving them money for a long enough time that they feel comfortable spending it. When I see this happening, it's time to head for the hills.

4. When brokerage firms continually declare record profits and you read that they have hired record numbers of new an-

alysts, get ready for a decline. Brokerage firms are absolutely the best contracyclical indicators around. If anyone should know better, you'd think it would be brokerage firms. There are some sharp firms, but, as a group, they are classically and consistently among the worst in their timing. Whenever you read that brokerage firms are expanding, opening new branches, entering all sorts of businesses they know nothing about, and hiring more brokers and analysts, it's time to get out of the marketplace. Conversely, when brokerage firms announce layoffs, record deficits, mass firings, and the closing of nonperforming branches, it may be time to reenter the market.

5. When all the investment newsletters that clutter your mailbox with junk mail tell you how fabulously they have done in the last couple of years, there's a reason. Because it's so easy to do well in a rising market (remember, half to five-eighths of the reason for success in the marketplace is simply *being in the market when it's rising*), most newsletter writers will of course achieve good performance. When dozens of them start crowing about their performance record, you know the party's over.

6. When *Investor's Intelligence* (a newsletter that monitors other investment newsletters) indicates that most newsletter writers are bearish, I'm certain I'm right around the beginning of the next move up. When *Investor's Intelligence* reports that most advisors are bullish, it's time to bid farewell.

7. When there is very heavy insider buying, I figure these corporate professionals, while they may not know a darn thing about the rest of the market, probably have a pretty good sense of what's going on in their own companies. Since most of them are proscribed by SEC rules from selling their stock short term, I feel pretty comfortable when thousands of them are buying shares of their own companies. This is another case where I wouldn't respond just because each of a number of individuals bought shares of one company, but over the broad range of American business, I find this a valid and valuable indicator. By the way, it's their actual buying I'm interested in; wouldn't give two cents for what they *say*. Of course, when thousands of insiders are selling their stocks, I also think that perhaps they know something about their individual company that I don't know. Again, they may just be selling for tax or other personal pur-

poses, but when *thousands* of them are selling, I get just a bit nervous.

8. When many odd-lotters are selling short and virtually no NYSE members are selling short, I've got a double whammy that tells me smart money is going long and people who have no business shorting are going short. This tells me it's probably time to buy. By the same token, when there's very little odd-lot short selling but lots and lots of members short selling, I think I should be interested in selling as well.

9. When all kinds of people are purchasing lots of puts and very few are purchasing calls, I figure it's time to buy. When lots of people are purchasing calls and nobody's buying puts, I figure it's time to sell. It's not that all these people are always wrong all the time, it's just that anybody dumb enough to spend any kind of money or time in the options market can't be too smart about figuring out its direction!

10. When mutual funds are under-invested, which is to say that they have very few investments relative to what they normally have and instead have a high percentage of cash reserves, that tells me I should be buying. By the same token, if they have no money in the form of cash reserves, that tells me they've been swept up in the euphoria of yet another market top and are virtually fully invested. They'll soon be selling their portfolio to meet investor demands for redemption and fueling the downward price spiral.

STALKING THE WILY INDICATORS

Where can all the above indicators be found? Between *Investor's Daily, Barron's* and *The Wall Street Journal* I can find virtually all this information, but I also let the coaches and advisors that I have hired in the form of newsletters do the work for me. If I ever get so nervous that I just can't wait to see the numbers every couple of weeks, I can always call the hot lines that many of these services offer. I know that they'll update their hot lines as necessary, because if they don't I and thousands like me will fire them.

Within the primary trends, there are often seasonal opportunities as well. Rather than go over these in detail, I'll refer you again to Yale Hirsch's *Stock Trader's Almanac*. Just to prove, however, that it never hurts to take a vacation from the marketplace, and that other opportunities will arise regularly, I'll discuss two situations that offer opportunities that you may want to take advantage of if you've missed the primary moves for some reason. There is no guarantee in these situations that history will repeat itself. Nonetheless, there are a couple of price behaviors that you may find interesting.

The first situation is the "four-year presidential cycle," which really does seem to exist. The stock market, more often than not, exhibits a weak first half in an election year, then a stronger second half. The year just after the election, in contrast, is virtually straight down, as is the first half of the next year. Then the second half of the third year is excellent, as is the first half of the final year in the cycle. Heading back into an election year, the last half of the fourth year is usually awful. If you're Pollyanna, you may believe that this is pure coincidence. If not, you may want to watch this usual pattern closely and benefit from the capriciousness of politicians and the short memories of investors—and voters.

As our second example of seasonal opportunities, gold-mining stocks reach a low point sometime at the end of the third quarter or during the fourth quarter of each year. Most of them then go on to reach their seasonal highs during the following spring or summer months. In some cases the resulting moves are nothing short of phenomenal. Does this mean that you should sell the farm and put all your marbles on this concept? By no means. It's meant merely to remind you that opportunities occasionally arise within the major moves.

Finally, we need to talk briefly about when to sell your stocks. People buy and sell for all sorts of crazy reasons. Chartists buy or sell because they think they see some pattern forming on their stock. Fundamentalists buy or sell because the company has changed its accounting measures and the fundamentalists didn't bother to read that but just saw a decline in earnings. Someone has a personal catastrophe and needs money. Someone else buys or sells because his or her astrological chart said that this is a propitious time to take action. Someone else gets a tip. Someone else gets disgruntled because the tip he or she got didn't work out. The chartists change their minds because they now realize they misinterpreted their charts and it was really a different pattern they saw. Someone else buys because the price has dropped and he or she now wants to average down, while yet another person buys because the price is going up and he or she now wants to pyramid up. For the most part, this is an irrational business. If you try to make sense of it, you'll be constantly frustrated. Better to accept it for what it is and enjoy the ride.

Lots of advisors will tell you what and when to buy. But how do you know when to sell? You sell your securities when the primary trend turns bad, and, if shorting, you short the weakest stocks in the weakest industries. Of course, there may be other times when you need to sell: when you need money, when you choose to break from the market to see which way things will shake out, when you believe the party's over for that stock, or when, upon reviewing it, you realize that if you had the choice to make today, you wouldn't buy that particular stock. Even if it's been very, very good to you, if you, looking at it with fresh eyes, say, "Gee, this thing looks awfully overpriced in here," you can be certain that other investors (those are the people you thought you were going to be selling that thing to) will be reaching the same conclusion. Selling into strength is the best way to go. That means that, after you've sold your stock, there's often still a lot of froth and fluff left in the marketplace. For this reason, you are not going to get the absolute high. Just because your stock goes up 5 or 6 points after you've sold, don't kick yourself for being crazy. If that's crazy, it's crazy like a fox. Remember, bulls make money, bears make money, but pigs never make money. By the same token, if you haven't heeded this advice and your stock is heading south, if the primary trend has been broken, get out of there! Not doing so is like refusing to parachute from a burning plane, even though the parachute will get you down safely, because you want to see how far the plane will go on its own power.

Tax selling is a particularly humorous (or sad) example of most people's unwillingness to make decisions. Many people procrastinate so completely that they hold on and hold on and hold on (even when they've already made the decision to sell for tax purposes) until December 31. How much sense does it take to realize that if you're doing this, so are 10 or 15 million other people? Guess what usually happens on December 31? Right— the price may not go down, but it seldom goes up enough to make it worthwhile to have held on.

Do you ever sell just to take a profit? Not unless you've made a decision that there's a better security that you want to be invested in at this time. Selling just to take a profit is doubly dumb. In addition to missing any future rise, you've now got all this money sloshing around that you just don't know what to do with so you often end up placing it in a more dubious issue.

You sell when the party's over, and you buy when it's time to party again. That's the secret of success in the stock market. There's nothing complicated about this. Do it and you'll win the investing decathlon. Ignore it, and you'll do nothing better than run with the pack. Many people derive psychological comfort from running with the pack. Believe me, there's even more psychological satisfaction in surrounding yourself with the rewards that distancing yourself from the pack can bring.

CHAPTER 14

BRINGING HOME THE GOLD—STARTING TODAY

What this investing game all comes down to is pretty straightforward. People fail in the market not because they don't understand complexities, but because they try to make it more complex than it is. All this hedging and straddling and stripping and strapping is tiresome work. Not only that, it's unnecessary work.

We've identified 10 simple keys.

Five winning strategies (Chapter 12):

1. Buying unpopular stocks of good companies.
2. Using convertible securities intelligently.
3. Selling short in bear markets.
4. Using warrants and warrant-like products.
5. Knowing when and how to use mutual funds.

. . . and five timing indicators (Chapter 13):

1. The dividend yield of the Dow Jones Industrials.
2. The book value of the Dow Jones Industrials.
3. The P/E ratio of the Dow Jones Industrials.
4. The actions of the Federal Reserve Board.
5. The mainstream opinions of the financial press.

Add to these the other five events in our decathlon in which we must be good enough to compete (Chapter 11) and the 10 secondary timing indicators (Chapter 13), and you've got it all. Combine the five winning events and the five timing tools alone and you'll break the tape. Put them all together and you'll be unstoppable.

Simple market truths don't change, and the reason is that

investor psychology doesn't change. From the Dutch tulip bulb craze of the 1600s onward, fear (of losing out or missing something) and greed (in the form of staying too long at the fair) have characterized the great mass of investors. Bernard Baruch put his finger on it in the 1920s, Gerald Loeb in the 1930s, and Fred Schwed, Jr., in the 1940s. A number of bright people have recognized these simple truths ever since, and it's up to you to decide whether you want to join them or not.

The last name I mentioned, Fred Schwed, Jr., is quoted by more people who either don't know it or don't admit it than almost anybody else in our business. Many people tell the story about the person who asked, upon being shown the yachts belonging to the brokers and bankers, "But where are the *customers'* yachts?" Fred Schwed, Jr., is the man who retold that story and used it as the title of his great 1940 book. In it he said,

> When the market is doing well and your friends and neighbors are buying stock, sell and put your money in the bank. [They didn't have money market funds when Schwed wrote his book.] The market will go higher—maybe quite a bit higher. Ignore it. Eventually there will be a recession. When it gets so bad as to arouse the politicians to make speeches, take your money out of the bank and buy stocks. The market will go lower—maybe quite a bit lower. Ignore it. This investment advice always works, but the procedure is so difficult that almost no one can do it.

Instead, what most people seem to seek is something like what is described in a book on the list at the back of this book called *Confessions of a Stock Broker,* written under the pseudonym Brutus. Brutus wrote his book "For the honestly unrealistic millions who are playing an unrealistic game. All they want is a stock that goes up 100% in a year, pays an 8% dividend while they wait, and has built-in guarantees against loss. Something conservative." If you're looking for this, you're out of control.

This book has been written for those who wish to take control. You have to be willing to hire smart coaches and trainers in the form of brokers, investment counselors, mutual fund managers, advisory services, and investment-newsletter writers. By hiring well, you're in control. You even "hire" a company's management for the time during which you hold shares of their securities (at least for purposes of your own portfolio). And it's up to you to fire each and every one of them if they don't work out.

You've got to take control by making the decision when to be in the market and when not to be in the market. Buy and hold? Nonsense! There's a time to be in competition and a time to rest between events.

You've also got to take control by going against the crowd. You're not in control when you're loping along at a pace that someone else is setting, running with the rest of the pack, living in blissful ignorance of the rewards that could be yours. You *are* in control when you make the active decision to leave the pack in the dust and break the tape. You *are* in control when you have the fortitude to think for yourself and to be flexible in your investment choices. The same kind of asset that served you well yesterday may not be the one that will serve you well tomorrow. Things change. The world changes. If we are really going from an industrial to an informational society, from a national economy to a global economy, from a centralized way of doing things to a decentralized way of doing things, from a noncomputerized to a computerized world, from a time when the number of consumers aged 18 to 24 were at an all-time high to a time, in just a few years, when those aged 35 to 44 will predominate and there will be a whole lot more people over 65, and from an industrial economy to a service economy, you've got to remain flexible. While not all these changes may come to pass, every one of them represents potentially wonderful investment opportunity. Only those willing to take control will benefit, however.

Want a little help in getting started distancing yourself from the pack? Take a look at some of the areas some smart investors are looking at. Utilities, especially the nuclear utilities, have had just about every kind of criticism and regulation thrown at them; there are those who believe that industry's next major move is likely to be in an upward direction.

How about the U.S. dollar? Can you think of anybody anywhere on the globe who loves the U.S. dollar? Just about every analyst in this country or elsewhere would rather be in West German marks or Japanese yen or Swiss francs or some other "strong" currency. Yes, it looks to the smart contrarian like a major bottom forming here—and what timing! Just as currency exchange warrants have become available to take advantage of a U.S. dollar rebound. . . .

Remember energy stocks? Those "buy them and forget them" stocks that everyone used to own back in the savage 1970s? This is a classic case of an industry with which the institutions have fallen out of love. You can buy the market *leaders* in this industry for what you paid for the absolute dogs a decade ago. If you believe the world might still need petroleum products in the coming years, you might just be one of the few who buy before everyone else decides oil stocks are the stocks to own.

This is what it all comes down to, competitors. Bernard Baruch, possibly the single most savvy investor of this century, said it best when he said, "I always buy my straw hats in the fall." He meant, of course, that the time to buy something is when no one else wants it. You could do worse than to buy your straw hat in the fall. If it flies off as you race to the finish line, never fear—one of those still in the pack behind you will stop to pick it up. And who knows? They'll probably even offer to buy it from you—for far more than you paid, of course.

It's in your hands, competitors. Bring home the gold!

SUGGESTED READING

Like this book? Read these.

I've listed them in quasi-chronological order so you can see that human nature hasn't changed much over the millennia. Some are "investment" books, but many are books about our competitors, those other humans making investment decisions—and, as such, may be more valuable in understanding greed, hope, fear, and despair than any book written specifically about the stock market.

1. *The Bible*

More greed, hope, fear, and despair than in any other book ever written. *Real* insights into human nature, especially in the Old Testament. Probably the Koran and other major world religions' books of knowledge have similar stories, but this is the one I'm most familiar with.

2. *Tao-Te Ching*

Written by Lao-Tze, who may have been a person or a people. Grand insights into the ways of nature, people, and self.

3. *Extraordinary Popular Delusions and the Madness of Crowds,* Charles Mackay

The Dutch tulip bulb fiasco, the Mississippi Company scam, the South Sea Bubble—it's all there. Read 'em and weep.

4. *Huckleberry Finn,* Mark Twain

The definitive American novel; shows just how hard they'll try to get you to conform and run with the pack.

5. *The Crowd,* Gustave Le Bon

So that's why they act the way they do. . . .

6. *Elmer Gantry,* Sinclair Lewis

Greed, hope, fear, and despair, updated for the twentieth century.

7. *The Battle for Investment Survival,* Gerald M. Loeb

Written a half-century ago (just eight years after *Elmer Gantry* said it in fictional form), and as relevant as if it had been written yesterday.

8. *Security Analysis: Principles and Techniques,* Benjamin Graham and David L. Dodd

What all of us cut our teeth on—and some of us move forward from. After 50+ years, there's still none better on the subject, except maybe Ben Graham's later effort, *The Intelligent Investor.*

9. *Where Are the Customers' Yachts?* Fred Schwed, Jr.

Pithy remarks, timeless wisdom. It seems the more things change, the more they stay the same.

10. *The Art of Contrary Thinking,* Humphrey Neill

A real troublemaker and rabble-rouser of the most wonderful kind. "Think for yourself"—what a concept!

11. *Common Stocks and Uncommon Profits,* Philip Fisher

Unlike many investment books, this one's text backs up the title.

12. *East of Eden,* John Steinbeck

Fear, greed, you know the rest. Does every generation have to discover this anew?

13. *Technical Analysis of Stock Trends,* Robert D. Edwards and John Magee

Love it or lampoon it, if you want to know about it, this is the book that'll teach you.

14. *Stan Weinstein's Secrets for Profiting in Bull and Bear Markets,* Stan Weinstein

If ever anyone could fill Edwards' and Magee's shoes, it's Stan. And Stan's book is easier to read.

15. *How to Buy Stocks,* Louis Engel (and, in recent editions, various gifted collaborators)

Absolutely the very best basic book on the market. Told with a certain breathless respect for the various institutions and traditions, but nonetheless a brilliant work for the market novice.

16. *Becket,* Jean Anouilh

Shows what happens when a single man tries to beat the government. Still, you have to wonder, who really lost, Henry or Becket?

17. *Why Most Investors Are Mostly Wrong Most of the Time,* William X. Scheinman

Well-researched, well-written, a wellspring. The title says it, the text explains it. Excellent.

18. *Money,* Lawrence S. Ritter and William L. Silber

Thank heavens, this is the first work I read on the subject. Judging by much of what I've seen since, I'd *still* be confused.

19. *Confessions of a Stockbroker,* "Brutus"

A view from the pit boss's side of the table.

20. *The Money Game,* "Adam Smith"

By the same tongue-in-cheek sage who later brought us *Supermoney* and others, this is destined to become a classic. Blinding insight into both the nature of the game and the players drawn to it.

21. *Stock Market Logic,* Norman G. Fosback

If you've always believed that "stock market logic" is as oxymoronic as "government aid" or "a good war," this book holds some very pleasant surprises.

22. *Contrary Investing,* Richard E. Band

Common-sense investing advice and lucid prose from a writer willing and able to see the forest *and* the trees—an unbeatable combination.

23. *Super Stocks,* Kenneth L. Fisher

From a money manager who always minds his ABCs and PSRs, a compelling look at the real fundamentals of investing.

24. *The Only Investment Guide You'll Ever Need,*
Andrew Tobias

A clever, thought-provoking, easy-to-read book that should be read along with *How to Buy Stocks.* As for its title: gee, I hope not. . . .

INDEX